KETO MEDITERRANEAN DIET COOKBOOK

1000 Days of Delicious Low-Carb, Heart-Healthy Recipes to Support Weight Loss, Boost Energy, and Enhance Longevity

VIOLA HARVEY

Contents

INTRODUCTION

Welcome to the *Keto-Mediterranean Diet Cookbook: 1000 Days of Delicious Low-Carb, Heart-Healthy Recipes to Support Weight Loss, Boost Energy, and Enhance Longevity, 21-Day Meal Plan for Optimal Results.* If you're looking to transform your health, enhance your energy, and enjoy delicious, satisfying meals, you've come to the right place. This book combines the best of both worlds—the scientifically-backed benefits of the ketogenic diet with the time-tested, heart-healthy practices of the Mediterranean lifestyle. Together, they create a powerful approach to health and wellness that can fit seamlessly into your life.

Overview of the Diet Combination

The Keto-Mediterranean diet brings together two popular and effective eating styles: the ketogenic diet and the Mediterranean diet. The ketogenic diet is renowned for its ability to promote weight loss, improve blood sugar control, and increase mental clarity by shifting the body into a state of ketosis, where it burns fat for fuel instead of carbohydrates. This low-carb, high-fat diet emphasizes the consumption of healthy fats, moderate protein, and minimal carbohydrates, making it a powerful tool for weight management and metabolic health.

On the other hand, the Mediterranean diet has been celebrated for centuries for its association with longevity, heart health, and overall well-being. It focuses on whole, unprocessed foods like fresh vegetables, fruits, lean proteins (especially fish), nuts, seeds, and olive oil. The Mediterranean diet encourages a balanced and mindful approach to eating, which includes enjoying meals with family and friends, savoring flavors, and prioritizing quality ingredients.

By combining these two approaches, the Keto-Mediterranean diet offers a synergistic effect that maximizes the benefits of each. You'll be adopting a low-carb, high-fat diet that supports ketosis, while also incorporating the nutrient-rich, anti-inflammatory foods typical of the Mediterranean diet. This fusion not only aids in weight loss but also supports heart health, brain function, and long-term wellness.

Benefits and Reasons for Combining Keto and Mediterranean Diets

The Keto-Mediterranean diet is more than just a way of eating; it's a lifestyle that brings a multitude of health benefits. Here are some compelling reasons to embrace this unique combination:

- **Weight Loss and Fat Burning:** By reducing carbohydrate intake and increasing healthy fats, the Keto-Mediterranean diet helps your body switch to burning fat for energy. This process not only promotes weight loss but also helps maintain muscle mass and supports a lean physique.
- **Heart Health:** The inclusion of olive oil, nuts, seeds, and fatty fish ensures that your diet is rich in heart-healthy omega-3 fatty acids. These fats help lower bad cholesterol (LDL) levels, reduce inflammation, and support overall cardiovascular health.
- **Improved Brain Function:** Healthy fats are essential for brain health. The Keto-Mediterranean diet provides a steady supply of energy to the brain, which can enhance mental clarity, focus, and cognitive function.
- **Longevity and Disease Prevention:** The Mediterranean aspect of the diet is associated with reduced risk of chronic diseases, including heart disease, cancer, and diabetes. When combined with the ketogenic approach, it creates a powerful defense against inflammation and oxidative stress, promoting longevity and overall vitality.
- **Stable Energy Levels:** By avoiding blood sugar spikes and crashes associated with high-carb diets, the Keto-Mediterranean diet provides stable, sustained energy throughout the day, helping you feel more vibrant and productive.

How to Use This Book

This cookbook is designed to be your comprehensive guide to adopting and thriving on the Keto-Mediterranean diet. Whether you're new to keto, a long-time follower of the Mediterranean diet, or just looking for a healthier way of eating, this book provides everything you need to succeed.

- **1000 Days of Recipes:** Inside, you'll find a variety of recipes that cater to different tastes, occasions, and dietary needs. From breakfast to dinner, snacks to desserts, each recipe is crafted to align with the principles of the Keto-Mediterranean diet. All recipes are low in carbohydrates, rich in healthy fats, and packed with flavor.
- **21-Day Meal Plan:** To help you get started, we've included a 21-day meal plan that takes the guesswork out of daily eating. This plan provides balanced, nutritious meals that will keep you satisfied, support your health goals, and introduce you to the versatility of the Keto-Mediterranean diet.
- **Nutritional Information:** Each recipe includes detailed nutritional information, helping you track your intake and stay within your dietary goals.
- **Tips and Guidelines:** Throughout the book, you'll find tips on how to adapt recipes, manage portion sizes, and make the diet work for your lifestyle. Whether you're dining out, hosting a dinner party, or looking for quick meal prep ideas, this book has you covered.

By choosing the Keto-Mediterranean diet, you're committing to a healthier, more balanced way of living. This cookbook is your companion on that journey, offering the tools, recipes, and inspiration you need to enjoy the process and see lasting results. Here's to delicious meals, improved health, and a lifetime of well-being. Welcome to the Keto-Mediterranean way of life!

UNDERSTANDING THE KETO-MEDITERRANEAN DIET

The Keto-Mediterranean diet is a unique approach that blends the principles of the ketogenic diet with the time-honored traditions of the Mediterranean diet. This fusion not only enhances the benefits of each diet but also makes it easier to maintain a healthy, balanced lifestyle. To fully appreciate how these two diets work together, let's explore what each one entails and why their combination can be so powerful.

The Ketogenic Diet: A Focus on Fat and Ketosis

The Keto-Mediterranean diet is a unique approach that blends the principles of the ketogenic diet with the time-honored traditions of the Mediterranean diet. This fusion not only enhances the benefits of each diet but also makes it easier to maintain a healthy, balanced lifestyle. To fully appreciate how these two diets work together, let's explore what each one entails and why their combination can be so powerful.

Key Components of the Ketogenic Diet:

Low Carbohydrates: Typically, keto restricts carbohydrate intake to about 20-50 grams per day, which forces the body to use fat as its primary energy source.

High Healthy Fats: Fats make up about 70-80% of the daily caloric intake in a keto diet. This includes sources like avocados, nuts, seeds, olive oil, and fatty fish.

Moderate Protein: Protein intake is moderate, around 20-25% of daily calories, to maintain muscle mass while not interfering with ketosis.

Benefits of the Ketogenic Diet:

Promotes weight loss by burning fat for energy
Improves blood sugar control and insulin sensitivity
Enhances mental clarity and focus
Reduces hunger and cravings by stabilizing blood sugar levels

The Mediterranean Diet: Heart-Healthy and Nutrient-Dense

The Mediterranean diet is inspired by the traditional eating habits of people living in Mediterranean regions, such as Greece, Italy, and Spain. It's widely recognized for its heart-healthy benefits and its role in promoting longevity. Unlike strict dieting, the Mediterranean approach is more about a lifestyle that includes balanced meals, enjoyment of food, and physical activity.

Key Components of the Mediterranean Diet:
- **Whole, Unprocessed Foods:** Focuses on fresh vegetables, fruits, whole grains, legumes, and lean proteins.
- **Healthy Fats:** Primarily uses olive oil as the main source of fat, along with nuts, seeds, and fatty fish.
- **Lean Proteins:** Emphasizes seafood, poultry, and plant-based proteins like legumes, with limited red meat consumption.
- **Moderate Dairy and Wine:** Includes moderate amounts of cheese, yogurt, and occasionally red wine.
- **Herbs and Spices:** Utilizes a variety of herbs and spices for flavor, reducing the need for added salt.

Benefits of the Mediterranean Diet:
- Supports heart health by reducing bad cholesterol levels
- Lowers the risk of chronic diseases, such as heart disease, diabetes, and cancer
- Promotes a healthy weight and improves metabolic health
- Encourages a holistic approach to eating and lifestyle

Why Combine Keto and Mediterranean Diets?

The Keto-Mediterranean diet combines the best of both worlds: the fat-burning benefits of keto with the heart-healthy, nutrient-rich foods of the Mediterranean diet. This fusion provides a balanced, sustainable way of eating that supports both short-term health goals and long-term wellness.

Enhanced Health Benefits:

Weight Loss: The low-carb nature of keto, combined with the satiating fats of the Mediterranean diet, helps in effective weight management and reduces the urge to overeat.

Heart Health: Incorporating Mediterranean staples like olive oil, nuts, seeds, and fatty fish ensures that the fats consumed are heart-healthy, supporting cardiovascular health while on keto.

Brain Health: The Omega-3 fatty acids from fish and anti-inflammatory properties of the Mediterranean diet can improve brain function and cognitive health, which is further supported by the stable energy supply from ketosis.

Longevity and Disease Prevention: This diet is rich in antioxidants, vitamins, and minerals from fresh vegetables, fruits, and healthy fats, which reduce inflammation and protect against chronic diseases.

How to Follow the Keto-Mediterranean Diet

Following the Keto-Mediterranean diet involves making food choices that align with both dietary principles. Here's a simple guide to help you get started:

- **Prioritize Healthy Fats:** Choose fats like olive oil, avocados, nuts, and seeds. Incorporate fatty fish like salmon, mackerel, and sardines regularly.
- **Limit Carbohydrates:** Keep your carb intake low, focusing on non-starchy vegetables like spinach, kale, zucchini, and broccoli. Avoid grains, sugars, and high-carb fruits.
- **Include Lean Proteins:** Opt for seafood, poultry, eggs, and plant-based proteins. Limit red meat and processed meats.
- **Enjoy Plenty of Vegetables:** Vegetables should be a central part of your diet. Choose a variety of colors and types to get a range of nutrients.
- **Moderate Dairy:** Include cheese and Greek yogurt in moderation, choosing full-fat options for better nutrient absorption and satiety.
- **Stay Hydrated:** Drink plenty of water and consider herbal teas. Stay away from sugary drinks and limit alcohol consumption.

A Lifestyle, Not a Diet

The Keto-Mediterranean diet is not just about the foods you eat—it's about enjoying a balanced lifestyle that promotes overall health. This includes taking time for meals, enjoying food with loved ones, staying active, and managing stress. By embracing this diet, you're not only working towards your health goals but also fostering a deeper appreciation for nutritious, delicious food.

This book is designed to guide you on this journey, providing you with the recipes, meal plans, and knowledge you need to thrive on the Keto-Mediterranean diet. Welcome to a healthier, happier way of living!

HISTORY AND ORIGINS OF THE KETOGENIC AND MEDITERRANEAN DIETS

The Ketogenic Diet

The ketogenic diet has its roots in medical science, dating back to the early 20th century. Originally developed in the 1920s by Dr. Russell Wilder at the Mayo Clinic, the diet was designed as a therapeutic approach to treat epilepsy, particularly in children. By mimicking the effects of fasting, the ketogenic diet helped control seizures when medications were ineffective. The diet's name comes from the production of ketones, substances produced by the liver when the body burns fat for energy instead of carbohydrates. Over the years, the ketogenic diet has gained popularity not only for epilepsy but also for its potential benefits in weight loss, diabetes management, and neurological health.

The Mediterranean Diet

The Mediterranean diet is rooted in the traditional eating habits of countries bordering the Mediterranean Sea, such as Greece, Italy, and Spain. This diet gained recognition in the mid-20th century when American scientist Ancel Keys conducted studies on the diet and its health impacts. His research highlighted the low incidence of heart disease among Mediterranean populations compared to other regions, despite their relatively high-fat diet. The Mediterranean diet emphasizes whole, unprocessed foods, including fruits, vegetables, whole grains, nuts, seeds, legumes, and olive oil, along with moderate consumption of fish, dairy, and wine. Its cultural emphasis on enjoyment of food, shared meals, and physical activity also plays a significant role in its health benefits.

Key Principles of Each Diet

Low Carbohydrate Intake: The ketogenic diet drastically reduces carbohydrate consumption, usually to about 20-50 grams per day, to induce a state of ketosis.

High Fat Intake: Healthy fats make up approximately 70-80% of daily caloric intake. This includes fats from sources like avocados, nuts, seeds, olive oil, and fatty fish.

Moderate Protein: Protein intake is kept moderate, typically around 20-25% of daily calories, to prevent the body from converting protein into glucose, which could interfere with ketosis.

Ketosis: The goal is to shift the body's metabolism from using glucose as the primary energy source to using fat, resulting in the production of ketones, which serve as an alternative energy source for the brain and muscles.

Key Principles of the Mediterranean Diet

Focus on Whole Foods: The Mediterranean diet emphasizes fresh, whole foods, such as fruits, vegetables, whole grains, legumes, nuts, and seeds.

Healthy Fats: Olive oil is the primary source of fat, used in cooking and salad dressings. Fatty fish, such as salmon and sardines, provide heart-healthy omega-3 fatty acids.

Moderate Protein from Lean Sources: The diet includes moderate amounts of fish, poultry, and plant-based proteins, with limited red meat consumption.

Rich in Fruits and Vegetables: A wide variety of fruits and vegetables are consumed daily, providing essential vitamins, minerals, and antioxidants.

Cultural and Social Aspects: Meals are often a social event, shared with family and friends. The diet encourages a balanced lifestyle that includes regular physical activity.

How They Complement Each Other

Combining the ketogenic and Mediterranean diets results in a powerful approach to health that takes advantage of the best aspects of both eating styles:

Healthy Fats from Both Diets: The emphasis on healthy fats from the ketogenic diet is perfectly aligned with the Mediterranean diet's use of olive oil, nuts, and fatty fish. This combination supports heart health, brain function, and inflammation reduction.

Low-Carb, High-Nutrient Vegetables: Both diets prioritize vegetables that are low in carbohydrates but high in nutrients, such as leafy greens, cruciferous vegetables, and tomatoes. This helps maintain ketosis while providing essential vitamins and minerals.

Quality Proteins: The inclusion of moderate amounts of lean proteins from fish, poultry, and plant sources, as found in the Mediterranean diet, aligns with the ketogenic diet's protein guidelines. This supports muscle maintenance and overall health.

Antioxidants and Anti-inflammatory Properties: The Mediterranean diet is rich in antioxidants from fruits, vegetables, and nuts, which complement the anti-inflammatory benefits of ketosis. Together, they help protect against chronic diseases and support long-term health.

Holistic Approach to Wellness: The Mediterranean lifestyle's focus on social connections, enjoyment of food, and physical activity complements the disciplined approach of the ketogenic diet, promoting overall well-being and sustainability.

Scientific Evidence and Health Benefits

Combining the ketogenic and Mediterranean diets can offer a wide range of health benefits, supported by scientific research:

Weight Loss: Studies have shown that low-carb diets like keto are effective for weight loss because they promote fat burning and reduce appetite. The Mediterranean diet's focus on whole, nutrient-dense foods supports satiety and weight management, making the combined approach effective for sustainable weight loss.

Heart Health: Research indicates that the Mediterranean diet reduces the risk of cardiovascular disease by lowering LDL cholesterol and triglyceride levels, thanks to healthy fats like olive oil and omega-3s from fish. The ketogenic diet also improves lipid profiles and promotes heart health by reducing inflammation and improving metabolic markers.

Blood Sugar Control: Both diets have been shown to improve insulin sensitivity and blood sugar levels. The ketogenic diet's low-carb approach minimizes glucose spikes, while the Mediterranean diet's emphasis on whole grains, fiber, and healthy fats supports steady blood sugar levels.

Cognitive Health: Ketosis provides a stable supply of energy to the brain, which can improve mental clarity and cognitive function. The Mediterranean diet's antioxidants and omega-3 fatty acids further support brain health, potentially reducing the risk of neurodegenerative diseases.

Longevity and Disease Prevention: The Mediterranean diet is associated with a reduced risk of chronic diseases like cancer and Alzheimer's, largely due to its anti-inflammatory and antioxidant properties. When combined with the ketogenic diet's benefits in reducing oxidative stress and inflammation, the Keto-Mediterranean diet offers a powerful approach to promoting longevity and overall health.

By understanding the origins, principles, and complementary nature of the ketogenic and Mediterranean diets, as well as the scientific evidence supporting their benefits, readers can appreciate the profound impact this combined dietary approach can have on their health and well-being. This book is your guide to making the Keto-Mediterranean diet a part of your daily life, unlocking its full potential to support weight loss, boost energy, and enhance longevity.

GETTING STARTED WITH THE KETO-MEDITERRANEAN DIET

Embarking on the Keto-Mediterranean diet journey is an exciting step toward improved health, weight management, and overall well-being. This section will guide you through the initial steps to ensure a smooth transition, help you stock your pantry with essential items, provide tips for grocery shopping, and recommend kitchen tools and equipment to make meal preparation easier and more enjoyable.

Transitioning to the Keto-Mediterranean Diet

Transitioning to the Keto-Mediterranean diet involves adjusting your eating habits and lifestyle to incorporate the key principles of both the ketogenic and Mediterranean diets. Here's how to get started:

- **Understand the Basics:** Begin by familiarizing yourself with the fundamental principles of the Keto-Mediterranean diet. This involves reducing carbohydrate intake to induce ketosis while emphasizing healthy fats and lean proteins typical of the Mediterranean diet. The goal is to shift your body from using glucose as its primary energy source to burning fat, which results in the production of ketones.
- **Gradual Reduction of Carbs:** If you're new to low-carb eating, it might be helpful to gradually reduce your carbohydrate intake instead of cutting it out all at once. Start by eliminating processed sugars, refined grains, and starchy foods like bread, pasta, and potatoes. Replace them with low-carb vegetables, healthy fats, and proteins.
- **Increase Healthy Fats**: Incorporate healthy fats into your meals, such as olive oil, avocados, nuts, seeds, and fatty fish. These fats will not only help you feel full and satisfied but also support ketosis and provide essential nutrients.
- **Prioritize Whole Foods:** Focus on whole, unprocessed foods. Fresh vegetables, lean proteins, and whole, unrefined fats should make up the majority of your meals. Avoid processed foods, which often contain hidden sugars and unhealthy fats.
- **Stay Hydrated:** The transition to a ketogenic state can lead to increased water loss. Drink plenty of water to stay hydrated, support digestion, and maintain overall health. Adding a pinch of salt to your water can help replenish lost electrolytes.
- **Listen to Your Body:** As your body adjusts to this new way of eating, you may experience temporary side effects such as fatigue, headaches, or irritability, often referred to as the "keto flu." These symptoms are normal and usually subside within a few days. Ensure you're consuming enough electrolytes and staying hydrated to alleviate these symptoms.
- **Meal Planning and Preparation:** Plan your meals ahead of time to ensure you have Keto-Mediterranean-friendly options available. Meal prepping can save time, reduce stress, and help you stick to your diet. Use the 21-day meal plan provided in this book as a starting point.

Essential Pantry Items

Stocking your pantry with the right ingredients is crucial for successfully following the Keto-Mediterranean diet. Here are some essential items to keep on hand:

Healthy Fats:
- Extra virgin olive oil (for cooking and dressings)
- Avocado oil
- Coconut oil
- Ghee or clarified butter
- Nuts and seeds (almonds, walnuts, chia seeds, flaxseeds)
- Nut butters (almond butter, tahini)

Proteins:
- Canned tuna or salmon
- Sardines and anchovies (great for salads and snacks)
- Canned chicken breast
- Canned legumes (chickpeas, lentils for occasional use)

Low-Carb Vegetables:
- Canned tomatoes (for sauces and stews)
- Artichoke hearts
- Olives (black and green)
- Pickles (sugar-free)
- Roasted red peppers

Baking Essentials:
- Almond flour
- Coconut flour
- Unsweetened cocoa powder
- Baking powder (look for aluminum-free)
- Stevia, erythritol, or monk fruit sweeteners (for baking and drinks)

Herbs and Spices:
- Oregano
- Basil
- Thyme
- Rosemary
- Cumin
- Paprika
- Garlic powder
- Onion powder
- Salt and pepper

Other Essentials:
- Vinegars (balsamic, apple cider, red wine vinegar)
- Mustard (Dijon, yellow)
- Soy sauce or tamari (for stir-fries)
- Broth (chicken, beef, or vegetable for soups and stews)
- Unsweetened almond milk or coconut milk (for smoothies and baking)

Grocery Shopping Tips

When shopping for the Keto-Mediterranean diet, it's important to make thoughtful choices that align with your dietary goals. Here are some tips to help you navigate the grocery store:

Shop the Perimeter: Most fresh, whole foods like vegetables, fruits, meats, and dairy are located around the perimeter of the store. Spend most of your time in these sections to avoid processed foods found in the middle aisles.

Read Labels Carefully: Always check the ingredient list and nutritional labels. Look out for added sugars, unhealthy oils, and artificial additives. Aim for products with simple, whole ingredients.

Choose Organic and Grass-Fed Options: When possible, opt for organic vegetables and grass-fed meats. These options are often higher in nutrients and free from harmful chemicals. Wild-caught fish is also a healthier choice than farm-raised.

Buy in Bulk: Stock up on pantry staples like nuts, seeds, and oils by buying in bulk. This can save money and ensure you always have healthy options on hand.

Fresh and Frozen Produce: Fresh vegetables are ideal, but don't overlook frozen options. Frozen vegetables are just as nutritious and can be a convenient way to add variety to your meals without worrying about spoilage.

Plan Ahead: Create a shopping list based on your weekly meal plan. This will help you stay organized, avoid impulse buys, and ensure you have all the ingredients needed to prepare your meals.

Kitchen Tools and Equipment

Equipping your kitchen with the right tools and equipment can make cooking on the Keto-Mediterranean diet easier and more enjoyable. Here are some essential items:

- **High-Quality Knives:** A good chef's knife and paring knife are essential for chopping vegetables, slicing meats, and preparing ingredients efficiently.
- **Cutting Boards:** Use separate cutting boards for meats and vegetables to avoid cross-contamination. Choose durable, easy-to-clean options.
- **Non-Stick Skillet and Sauté Pan:** These are perfect for cooking eggs, vegetables, and lean proteins without sticking. Look for pans with a non-toxic coating.
- **Cast Iron Skillet:** A versatile tool that can be used for searing, baking, and roasting. It retains heat well and adds a unique flavor to your dishes.
- **Blender or Food Processor:** Essential for making smoothies, sauces, dressings, and keto-friendly desserts. A food processor is particularly useful for making cauliflower rice or nut butters.
- **Spiralizer:** A spiralizer can turn vegetables like zucchini and carrots into noodle-like strands, perfect for low-carb pasta alternatives.
- **Baking Sheets and Muffin Tins:** These are useful for roasting vegetables, baking keto-friendly bread, and making muffins or egg cups.
- **Slow Cooker or Instant Pot:** These appliances are great for preparing hearty stews, soups, and slow-cooked meats with minimal effort. They save time and can make meal prep easier.
- **Measuring Cups and Spoons:** Accurate measurements are important for following recipes, especially when it comes to baking and maintaining portion control.
- **Digital Kitchen Scale:** A scale helps ensure accuracy when measuring ingredients, especially for those closely tracking their macronutrient intake.

Getting started with the Keto-Mediterranean diet involves some preparation and planning, but it's a rewarding journey toward better health and well-being. By transitioning gradually, stocking your pantry with essential items, shopping wisely, and equipping your kitchen with the right tools, you'll set yourself up for success. With these foundations in place, you can fully embrace the Keto-Mediterranean lifestyle and enjoy the many benefits it offers.

BREAKFAST

AVOCADO AND EGG BOATS

PREP TIME:
5 MINS

COOK TIME:
15 MINS

TOTAL TIME:
20 MINS

SERVING
2

Nutrition

Calories: 300, Protein: 10g,
Carbohydrate: 12g, Fat: 25g

INGREDIENTS

- 2 ripe avocados
- 4 small eggs
- Salt and pepper to taste
- 1 tablespoon olive oil
- 1 teaspoon chopped fresh chives (optional)
- 1 teaspoon chopped fresh parsley (optional)
- 1/2 teaspoon red pepper flakes (optional)

INSTRUCTIONS

1. Preheat oven to 375°F (190°C). Cut the avocados in half to discard the pits. Scoop out some flesh to create a larger well for the eggs.
2. Place the avocado pieces in a baking dish, ensuring they are stable. If needed, you can use crumpled foil to help stabilize them.
3. Crack an egg into each half. Powder with salt and crushed pepper.
4. Drizzle the olive oil over the eggs and avocados.
5. Bake for 12-15 minutes until the eggs are cooked to your desired level of doneness.
6. Remove and sprinkle with chopped chives, parsley, and red pepper flakes if using. Serve immediately.

CHIA SEED PUDDING WITH ALMONDS

PREP TIME:
5 MINS

COOK TIME:
00 MINS

TOTAL TIME:
5 MINS

SERVING
2

Nutrition

Calories: 180, Protein: 5g,
Carbohydrate: 10g, Fat: 12g

INGREDIENTS

- 1/4 cup chia seeds
- 1 cup unsweetened almond milk
- 1 teaspoon vanilla extract
- A few drops of liquid stevia (optional)
- 2 tablespoons sliced almonds
- 1/4 cup fresh berries (optional)

INSTRUCTIONS

1. Toss the chia seeds, almond milk, vanilla extract, and stevia in a deep-bottom bowl.
2. Cover and refrigerate for 4 hours (at least) or overnight until the mixture thickens to a pudding-like consistency.
3. Before serving, stir the pudding to ensure it is well-mixed. Divide the pudding between two bowls. Top with almond slices and fresh berries if desired. Serve chilled.

MEDITERRANEAN OMELET WITH SUN-DRIED TOMATOES

PREP TIME:
5 MINS

COOK TIME:
10 MINS

TOTAL TIME:
15 MINS

SERVING
1

Nutrition

Calories: 350, Protein: 18g,
Carbohydrate: 6g, Fat: 28g

INGREDIENTS

- 3 large eggs
- 1/4 cup oil-packed chopped sun-dried tomatoes (drained)
- 1/4 cup crumbled feta cheese
- 1/4 cup fresh spinach, chopped
- 1 tablespoon olive oil
- Salt and pepper to taste

INSTRUCTIONS

1. In a deep-bottom bowl, whisk the eggs with salt and pepper.
2. Heat one tbsp oil in a non-stick skillet over medium stove heat.
3. Add oil-packed tomatoes and spinach to the skillet and sauté for 2-3 minutes.
4. Ladle the pulsed eggs over the vegetables and cook until the edges start to set.
5. Sprinkle the feta cheese on top. Fold the omelet and keep cooking until the eggs are fully set. Serve immediately.

BAKED EGGS WITH SPINACH AND FETA

PREP TIME:
5 MINS

COOK TIME:
15 MINS

TOTAL TIME:
20 MINS

SERVING
2

Nutrition

Calories: 250, Protein: 16g,
Carbohydrate: 4g, Fat: 20g

INGREDIENTS

- 4 large eggs
- 1 cup fresh spinach, chopped
- 1/4 cup crumbled feta cheese
- 2 tablespoons heavy cream
- 1 tablespoon olive oil
- Salt and pepper to taste

INSTRUCTIONS

1. Preheat oven to 375°F (190°C). Grease two small ovenproof dishes with one tbsp oil. Divide the chopped spinach between the two dishes.
2. Crack two eggs into each dish over the spinach. Drizzle each dish with 1 tablespoon of heavy cream.
3. Sprinkle with feta cheese, salt, and pepper. Bake for 12-15 minutes or until the eggs are set to your liking. Serve immediately.

KETO GREEK YOGURT PARFAIT

PREP TIME:
5 MINS

COOK TIME:
00 MINS

TOTAL TIME:
5 MINS

SERVING
2

Nutrition

Calories: 200, Protein: 10g,
Carbohydrate: 15g, Fat: 12g

INGREDIENTS

- 1 cup full-fat Greek yogurt
- 1/2 cup mixed berries (strawberries, blueberries, raspberries)
- 2 tablespoons chopped almonds
- 2 tablespoons unsweetened shredded coconut
- 1 teaspoon vanilla extract
- A few drops of liquid stevia (optional)

INSTRUCTIONS

1. In a deep-bottom bowl, mix the Greek yogurt and vanilla extract. Add stevia if desired.
2. Divide the vanilla yogurt mixture between two serving bowls.
3. Top each bowl with mixed berries, chopped almonds, and shredded coconut.
4. Serve immediately.

MEDITERRANEAN SPICED SHAKSHUKA

PREP TIME:
10 MINS

COOK TIME:
20 MINS

TOTAL TIME:
30 MINS

SERVING
4

Nutrition

Calories: 150, Protein: 8g,
Carbohydrate: 12g, Fat: 8g

INGREDIENTS

- 1 tablespoon olive oil
- 1 onion, diced
- 1 red bell pepper, diced
- 2 cloves garlic, minced
- 1 teaspoon ground cumin
- 1 teaspoon paprika
- 1/2 teaspoon ground coriander
- 1/4 teaspoon chili powder
- 1 can (14 oz) diced tomatoes
- 4 large eggs
- Salt and pepper to taste
- Fresh parsley, chopped (for garnish)

INSTRUCTIONS

1. Heat one tbsp oil in a skillet over medium stove heat. Add diced onion and bell pepper, and sauté until softened.
2. Add garlic, cumin, paprika, coriander, and chili powder. Cook for another 1-2 minutes. Ladle in the diced tomatoes, Powder with salt and crushed pepper, and simmer for 10 minutes.
3. Create four wells in the tomato mixture and crack one egg into each. Cover the skillet and cook to your liking. Spread fresh parsley to garnish on top and serve immediately.

FLAXSEED PORRIDGE WITH BERRIES

PREP TIME:
5 MINS

COOK TIME:
5 MINS

TOTAL TIME:
10 MINS

SERVING
2

Nutrition

Calories: 200, Protein: 6g,
Carbohydrate: 12g, Fat: 16g

INGREDIENTS

- 1/2 cup ground flaxseed
- 1 cup unsweetened almond milk
- 1 teaspoon vanilla extract
- A few drops of liquid stevia (optional)
- ½ cup mixed berries (strawberries, blueberries, raspberries)
- 2 tablespoons chopped almonds (optional)

INSTRUCTIONS

1. In a saucepan, combine the ground flaxseed, almond milk, vanilla extract, and stevia if using.
2. Cook over medium stove heat, stirring frequently, until the mixture thickens, about 3-5 minutes.
3. Divide the porridge between two bowls. Top with mixed berries and chopped almonds.

GREEK-INSPIRED SCRAMBLED EGGS

PREP TIME:
5 MINS

COOK TIME:
5 MINS

TOTAL TIME:
10 MINS

SERVING
1

Nutrition

Calories: 300, Protein: 18g,
Carbohydrate: 3g, Fat: 24g

INGREDIENTS

- 3 large eggs
- 1/4 cup crumbled feta cheese
- 1/4 cup chopped spinach
- 1 tablespoon olive oil
- Salt and pepper to taste
- 1 tablespoon chopped fresh parsley (optional)

INSTRUCTIONS

1. In a deep-bottom bowl, whisk the eggs with salt and pepper. Heat one tbsp oil in a non-stick skillet over medium stove heat.
2. Add chopped spinach and leave to cook until wilted. Drop the beaten eggs into the skillet and scramble until just set.
3. Toss in the crumbled feta cheese. Remove and sprinkle with fresh parsley if desired.
4. Serve immediately.

LEMON RICOTTA PANCAKES

PREP TIME:
10 MINS

COOK TIME:
15 MINS

TOTAL TIME:
25 MINS

SERVING
2

Nutrition

Calories: 300, Protein: 14g,
Carbohydrate: 12g, Fat: 24g

INGREDIENTS

- 1 cup almond flour
- 1/2 cup ricotta cheese
- 2 large eggs
- 1/4 cup unsweetened almond milk
- 1 teaspoon lemon zest
- 1 teaspoon vanilla extract
- 1/2 teaspoon baking powder
- Pinch of salt
- 1 tablespoon olive oil (for cooking)
- 1/2 cup fresh berries (for topping)

INSTRUCTIONS

1. In a deep-bottom bowl, mix almond flour, ricotta cheese, eggs, almond milk, lemon zest, vanilla extract, baking powder, and salt until well combined.
2. Heat one tbsp oil in a non-stick skillet over medium stove heat.
3. Pour batter (just a small amount) into the skillet to form pancakes. Cook until bubble appears on the upper surface, then flip and cook until golden brown.
4. Serve the pancakes topped with fresh berries.

PROSCIUTTO-WRAPPED ASPARAGUS WITH EGGS

PREP TIME:
10 MINS

COOK TIME:
15 MINS

TOTAL TIME:
25 MINS

SERVING
2

Nutrition

Calories: 250, Protein: 18g,
Carbohydrate: 5g, Fat: 18g

INGREDIENTS

- 12 asparagus spears
- 6 slices of prosciutto
- 4 large eggs
- 1 tablespoon olive oil
- Salt and pepper to taste
- Fresh parsley, chopped (optional)

INSTRUCTIONS

1. Preheat oven to 400°F (200°C). Wrap each asparagus spear with a prosciutto slice.
2. Place the wrapped asparagus on the paper-arranged baking sheet and drizzle one tbsp oil.
3. Bake for 12-15 minutes until the prosciutto is crispy. While baking, poach or fry the eggs to your liking.
4. Serve the prosciutto-wrapped asparagus with the eggs on top. Spread fresh parsley if desired. Serve immediately.

KETO CAULIFLOWER BREAKFAST HASH

PREP TIME:
10 MINS

COOK TIME:
15 MINS

TOTAL TIME:
25 MINS

SERVING
2

Nutrition

Calories: 300, Protein: 14g,
Carbohydrate: 12g, Fat: 24g

INGREDIENTS

- 2 cups riced cauliflower
- 1/2 cup diced bell pepper
- 1/2 cup diced onion
- 2 cloves garlic, minced
- 4 large eggs
- 2 tablespoons olive oil
- 1/4 teaspoon paprika
- Salt and pepper to taste
- Fresh parsley, chopped (optional)

INSTRUCTIONS

1. Heat one tbsp oil in a skillet over medium stove heat. Add diced bell pepper, onion, and garlic to the skillet and sauté until softened, about 5 minutes.
2. Add rice cauliflower and cook for 5 minutes, until tender. Powder it with paprika, salt, and crushed pepper.
3. In a separate skillet, heat the leftover oil and cook the eggs to your like (fried or scrambled).
4. Serve the cauliflower hash topped with the cooked eggs and spread fresh parsley on topif desired.

LUNCH

SMOKED SALMON AND AVOCADO SALAD

PREP TIME:
10 MINS

COOK TIME:
00 MINS

TOTAL TIME:
10 MINS

SERVING
2

Nutrition

Calories: 300, Protein: 12g,
Carbohydrate: 10g, Fat: 24g

INGREDIENTS

- 4 ounces smoked salmon, sliced
- 1 avocado, sliced
- 2 cups mixed greens
- 1/4 red onion, thinly sliced
- 1 tablespoon capers
- 1 tablespoon olive oil
- 1 teaspoon lemon juice
- Salt and pepper to taste

INSTRUCTIONS

1. In the deep-bottom bowl, combine the mixed greens, smoked salmon, avocado, red onion, and capers.
2. In a small, deep-bottom bowl, toss the oil with lemon juice, salt, and crushed pepper.
3. Drizzle the lemon-oil dressing over the salad and toss gently to combine.
4. Serve immediately.

GRILLED CHICKEN SALAD WITH OLIVE OIL DRESSING

PREP TIME:
15 MINS

COOK TIME:
15 MINS

TOTAL TIME:
30 MINS

SERVING
2

Nutrition

Calories: 350, Protein: 30g,
Carbohydrate: 12g, Fat: 20g

INGREDIENTS

- 2 boneless, skinless chicken breasts
- 4 cups mixed greens
- 1 cucumber, sliced
- 1/2 cup cherry tomatoes, halved
- 1/4 cup red onion, thinly sliced
- 1/4 cup Kalamata olives
- 2 tablespoons feta cheese, crumbled
- 2 tablespoons olive oil
- 1 tablespoon red wine vinegar
- 1 teaspoon dried oregano
- Salt and pepper to taste

INSTRUCTIONS

1. Preheat the grill to medium-high heat. Massage the breast meat with salt, crushed pepper, and half of the dried oregano.
2. Grill the chicken for 6-7 minutes on one side until fully cooked. Let rest for a few minutes before slicing.
3. In the deep-bottom bowl, combine the mixed greens, cucumber, cherry tomatoes, red onion, and olives.
4. In a small, deep-bottom bowl, toss the oil with red wine vinegar, remaining oregano, salt, and crushed pepper.
5. Drizzle the vinegar-oil dressing over the salad and toss to combine. Put the sliced grilled chicken over the salad bed and sprinkle with feta cheese. Serve immediately.

ZUCCHINI NOODLES WITH PESTO AND PINE NUTS

PREP TIME:
10 MINS

COOK TIME:
5 MINS

TOTAL TIME:
15 MINS

SERVING
2

Nutrition

Calories: 250, Protein: 8g,
Carbohydrate: 8g, Fat: 20g

INGREDIENTS

- 2 medium zucchinis, spiralized
- 1/4 cup pesto sauce
- 2 tablespoons pine nuts, toasted
- 1 tablespoon olive oil
- 1/4 cup grated Parmesan cheese
- Salt and pepper to taste

INSTRUCTIONS

1. Heat one tbsp oil in a skillet over medium stove heat.
2. Add zucchini noodles and sauté for 2-3 minutes, until just tender.
3. Remove from heat and toss with the pesto sauce.
4. Divide the zucchini noodles between two plates.
5. Top with toasted pine nuts with grated Parmesan cheese.
6. Powder it with salt and crushed pepper to taste.
7. Serve immediately.

GREEK SALAD WITH GRILLED SHRIMP

PREP TIME:
15 MINS

COOK TIME:
10 MINS

TOTAL TIME:
25 MINS

SERVING
2

Nutrition

Calories: 300, Protein: 24g,
Carbohydrate: 10g, Fat: 20g

INGREDIENTS

- 12 large shrimp, peeled and deveined
- 4 cups romaine lettuce, chopped
- 1 cucumber, diced
- 1/2 cup cherry tomatoes, halved
- 1/4 cup red onion, thinly sliced
- 1/4 cup Kalamata olives, pitted
- 1/4 cup feta cheese, crumbled
- 2 tablespoons olive oil
- 1 tablespoon lemon juice
- 1 teaspoon dried oregano
- Salt and pepper to taste

INSTRUCTIONS

1. Preheat the grill to medium-high heat.
2. In a small, deep-bottom bowl, toss the shrimp with one tbsp oil, lemon juice, oregano, salt, and crushed pepper.
3. Grill the shrimp for 2-3 minutes for one side, or until opaque and cooked through. Set aside.
4. In the deep-bottom bowl, combine the romaine lettuce, cucumber, cherry tomatoes, red onion, and olives.
5. In a small, deep-bottom bowl, toss the leftover oil with lemon juice, salt, and crushed pepper.
6. Drizzle the lemon-oil dressing over the salad and toss to combine.
7. Top the salad with grilled shrimp and sprinkle with feta cheese.
8. Serve immediately.

CAULIFLOWER TABOULEH

PREP TIME:
15 MINS

COOK TIME:
5 MINS

TOTAL TIME:
20 MINS

SERVING
4

Nutrition

Calories: 120, Protein: 2g,
Carbohydrate: 10g, Fat: 9g

INGREDIENTS

- 1 small head cauliflower, riced
- 1 cup chopped parsley
- 1/2 cup chopped mint
- 1/2 cup diced cucumber
- 1/2 cup diced tomatoes
- 1/4 cup diced red onion
- 1/4 cup olive oil
- 2 tablespoons lemon juice
- Salt and pepper to taste

INSTRUCTIONS

1. Steam the riced cauliflower for 3-5 minutes until tender. Let cool.
2. Combine the cauliflower, parsley, mint, cucumber, tomatoes, and red onion in a deep-bottom bowl.
3. In a small, deep-bottom bowl, toss the oil with lemon juice, salt, and crushed pepper.
4. Pour the lemon-oil dressing over the cauliflower mixture and toss to combine.
5. Serve chilled.

SPINACH AND FETA STUFFED CHICKEN BREAST

PREP TIME:
10 MINS

COOK TIME:
25 MINS

TOTAL TIME:
35 MINS

SERVING
2

Nutrition

Calories: 300, Protein: 40g,
Carbohydrate: 3g, Fat: 15g

INGREDIENTS

- 2 boneless, skinless chicken breasts
- 1 cup fresh spinach, chopped
- 1/4 cup crumbled feta cheese
- 1 tablespoon olive oil
- 1 teaspoon garlic powder
- Salt and pepper to taste

INSTRUCTIONS

1. Preheat oven to 375°F (190°C).
2. Make the slit into the side of each breast meat to create a pocket.
3. In a bowl, mix the chopped spinach and feta cheese.
4. Stuff the breast meat with the spinach and feta mixture. Secure with toothpicks if necessary.
5. Rub the chicken with one tbsp oil, garlic powder, salt, and crushed pepper.
6. Place the chicken in a baking dish and bake for 27-30 minutes until fully cooked.
7. Remove toothpicks before serving. Serve immediately.

MEDITERRANEAN TURKEY MEATBALLS

PREP TIME:
15 MINS

COOK TIME:
20 MINS

TOTAL TIME:
35 MINS

SERVING
4

Nutrition

Calories: 250, Protein: 22g,
Carbohydrate: 4g, Fat: 15g

INGREDIENTS

- 1 pound ground turkey
- 1/4 cup crumbled feta cheese
- 1/4 cup chopped parsley
- 1/4 cup almond flour
- 1 egg
- 2 cloves garlic, minced
- 1 teaspoon dried oregano
- Salt and pepper to taste
- 2 tablespoons olive oil

INSTRUCTIONS

1. Preheat oven to 400°F (200°C).
2. In the deep-bottom bowl, combine the ground turkey, feta cheese, parsley, almond flour, egg, garlic, oregano, salt, and crushed pepper. Mix well.
3. Form the mixture into small meatballs.
4. Heat two tbsp oil in a skillet over medium stove heat. Brown the meatballs on all sides.
5. Transfer the meatballs to the paper-arranged baking sheet and bake for 17-20 minutes.
6. Serve immediately.

TUNA AND OLIVE SALAD

PREP TIME:
10 MINS

COOK TIME:
00 MINS

TOTAL TIME:
10 MINS

SERVING
2

Nutrition

Calories: 250, Protein: 20g,
Carbohydrate: 8g, Fat: 16g

INGREDIENTS

- 1 can (5 oz) tuna in olive oil, drained
- 1/2 cup mixed olives, pitted and halved
- 1/2 cup cherry tomatoes, halved
- 1/4 cup diced red onion
- 2 cups mixed greens
- 2 tablespoons olive oil
- 1 tablespoon lemon juice
- Salt and pepper to taste

INSTRUCTIONS

1. In the deep-bottom bowl, combine the tuna, olives, cherry tomatoes, red onion, and mixed greens.
2. In a small, deep-bottom bowl, toss the oil with lemon juice, salt, and crushed pepper.
3. Drizzle the lemon-oil dressing over the salad and toss gently to combine.
4. Serve immediately.

LEMON HERB CHICKEN SALAD

PREP TIME:
15 MINS

COOK TIME:
20 MINS

TOTAL TIME:
35 MINS

SERVING
2

Nutrition

Calories: 350, Protein: 30g,
Carbohydrate: 10g, Fat: 20g

INGREDIENTS

- 2 boneless, skinless chicken breasts
- 2 tablespoons olive oil
- 1 tablespoon lemon juice
- 1 teaspoon dried oregano
- 1 teaspoon dried thyme
- Salt and pepper to taste
- 4 cups mixed greens
- 1/2 cup cherry tomatoes, halved
- 1/2 cucumber, sliced
- 1/4 red onion, thinly sliced
- 1/4 cup crumbled feta cheese

INSTRUCTIONS

1. Preheat the grill or a skillet over medium stove heat.
2. In a small, deep-bottom bowl, mix one tbsp oil, lemon juice, oregano, thyme, salt, and crushed pepper. Rub the mixture over the chicken breasts.
3. Grill or cook the chicken for 6-7 minutes for one side or until fully cooked. Let rest before slicing.
4. In the deep-bottom bowl, combine mixed greens, cherry tomatoes, cucumber, and red onion.
5. Slice the breast and add to the salad.
6. Drizzle the two tbsp oil and toss to combine.
7. Sprinkle with crumbled cheese and serve immediately.

SHRIMP AND AVOCADO SALAD

 PREP TIME:
10 MINS

 COOK TIME:
5 MINS

 TOTAL TIME:
15 MINS

 SERVING
2

Nutrition

Calories: 300, Protein: 20g,
Carbohydrate: 10g, Fat: 22g

INGREDIENTS

- 12 large shrimp, peeled and deveined
- 1 tablespoon olive oil
- 1 avocado, sliced
- 2 cups mixed greens
- 1/2 cup cherry tomatoes, halved
- 1/4 cup red onion, thinly sliced
- 1 tablespoon lemon juice
- 1 tablespoon olive oil (for dressing)
- Salt and pepper to taste

INSTRUCTIONS

1. Heat one tbsp oil in a skillet over medium stove heat. Add shrimp and cook for 2-3 minutes for one side until pink and opaque. Remove from heat.
2. In the deep-bottom bowl, combine the mixed greens, cherry tomatoes, red onion, and avocado.
3. Add the cooked shrimp on top of the salad.
4. In a small deep-bottom bowl, toss the lemon juice, 1 tablespoon olive oil, salt, and crushed pepper.
5. Drizzle lemon-oil dressing over the salad and toss gently to combine.
6. Serve immediately.

MEDITERRANEAN CAULIFLOWER COUSCOUS

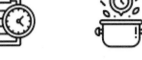

PREP TIME:
15 MINS

COOK TIME:
5 MINS

TOTAL TIME:
20 MINS

SERVING
4

Nutrition

Calories: 120, Protein: 3g,
Carbohydrate: 8g, Fat: 10g

INGREDIENTS

- 1 small head cauliflower, riced
- 1/4 cup chopped fresh parsley
- 1/4 cup chopped fresh mint
- 1/2 cup diced cucumber
- 1/2 cup diced tomatoes
- 1/4 cup diced red onion
- 1/4 cup sliced pitted Kalamata olives
- 2 tablespoons olive oil
- 2 tablespoons lemon juice
- Salt and pepper to taste

INSTRUCTIONS

1. Steam the riced cauliflower for 3-5 minutes until tender. Let cool.
2. Combine the cauliflower, parsley, mint, cucumber, tomatoes, red onion, and olives in a deep-bottom bowl.
3. In a small, deep-bottom bowl, toss the oil with lemon juice, salt, and crushed pepper.
4. Pour the lemon-oil dressing over the cauliflower mixture and toss to combine.
5. Serve chilled or at room temperature.

KETO LAMB KOFTA

PREP TIME:
15 MINS

COOK TIME:
100 MINS

TOTAL TIME:
25 MINS

SERVING
4

Nutrition

Calories: 250, Protein: 20g,
Carbohydrate: 2g, Fat: 18g

INGREDIENTS

- 1 pound ground lamb
- 1/4 cup chopped fresh parsley
- 1/4 cup chopped fresh mint
- 2 cloves garlic, minced
- 1 teaspoon ground cumin
- 1 teaspoon ground coriander
- 1/2 teaspoon ground cinnamon
- Salt and pepper to taste
- 2 tablespoons olive oil

INSTRUCTIONS

1. In the deep-bottom bowl, combine the ground lamb, parsley, mint, garlic, cumin, coriander, cinnamon, salt, and crushed pepper. Mix well.
2. Form the mixture into small patties or logs.
3. Heat two tbsp oil in a skillet over medium stove heat. Cook the kofta for 3-4 minutes on one side or until fully cooked. Serve immediately.

DINNER

BAKED SALMON WITH ASPARAGUS AND LEMON

PREP TIME:
10 MINS

COOK TIME:
15 MINS

TOTAL TIME:
25 MINS

SERVING
2

Nutrition

Calories: 350, Protein: 28g,
Carbohydrate: 8g, Fat: 24g

INGREDIENTS

- 2 salmon fillets
- 1 bunch asparagus, trimmed
- 2 tablespoons olive oil
- 1 lemon, thinly sliced
- 2 cloves garlic, minced
- Salt and pepper to taste
- Fresh parsley, chopped (for garnish)

INSTRUCTIONS

1. Preheat oven to 400°F (200°C). Place the salmon fillets and asparagus on the paper-arranged baking sheet.
2. Drizzle two tbsp oil and sprinkle with minced garlic, salt, and crushed pepper. Top the salmon with lemon slices.
3. Bake for 12-15 minutes until the fish is done thoroughly and the asparagus is tender. Garnish with fresh parsley before serving. Serve immediately.

LAMB CHOPS WITH MINT PESTO

PREP TIME:
10 MINS

COOK TIME:
15 MINS

TOTAL TIME:
25 MINS

SERVING
4

Nutrition

Calories: 400, Protein: 24g,
Carbohydrate: 4g, Fat: 34g

INGREDIENTS

- 8 lamb chops
- 2 tablespoons olive oil
- Salt and pepper to taste
- Mint Pesto:
- 1 cup fresh mint leaves
- 1/4 cup fresh parsley
- 1/4 cup pine nuts
- 1/4 cup grated Parmesan cheese
- 2 cloves garlic
- 1/2 cup olive oil
- Salt and pepper to taste

INSTRUCTIONS

1. Preheat your grill or skillet over medium stove heat. Powder the lamb chops with olive oil, salt, and crushed pepper.
2. Grill the lamb chops for 3-4 minutes for one side or until cooked to your liking. Remove from heat and let rest.
3. For the mint pesto, combine mint leaves, parsley, pine nuts, Parmesan cheese, garlic, 1/2 cup oil, salt, and crushed pepper in a food blender. Blend until smooth.
4. Serve the lamb chops with mint pesto on the side.

MEDITERRANEAN CHICKEN SKEWERS

PREP TIME:
20 MINS

COOK TIME:
15 MINS

TOTAL TIME:
35 MINS

SERVING
4

Nutrition

Calories: 280, Protein: 24g,
Carbohydrate: 8g, Fat: 18g

INGREDIENTS

- 2 chicken breasts (without skin & bone) cut into cubes
- 1 red bell pepper, cut into squares
- 1 yellow bell pepper, cut into squares
- 1 red onion, cut into squares
- 1/4 cup olive oil
- 2 tablespoons lemon juice
- 2 cloves garlic, minced
- 1 teaspoon dried oregano
- 1 teaspoon dried thyme
- Salt and pepper to taste
- Wooden skewers (soaked in water (duration 30 minutes) to avoid burn)

INSTRUCTIONS

1. In a deep-bottom bowl, mix olive oil, lemon juice, garlic, oregano, thyme, salt, and crushed pepper.
2. Add the chicken cubes, bell peppers, and onion to the bowl. Toss to coat evenly. Marinate for at least 15 minutes.
3. Preheat the grill or skillet over medium stove heat. Thread the meat & veggies onto the skewers.
4. Grill the skewers for 12-15 minutes, turning from time to time, until the chicken is fully cooked and the vegetables are tender. Serve immediately.

RATATOUILLE WITH A KETO TWIST

PREP TIME:
15 MINS

COOK TIME:
30 MINS

TOTAL TIME:
45 MINS

SERVING
4

Nutrition

Calories: 150, Protein: 3g,
Carbohydrate: 12g, Fat: 10g

INGREDIENTS

- 1 small eggplant, diced
- 1 zucchini, diced
- 1 yellow squash, diced
- 1 red bell pepper, diced
- 1 yellow bell pepper, diced
- 1 small onion, diced
- 2 cloves garlic, minced
- 1 can (14 oz) diced tomatoes
- 1/4 cup olive oil
- 1 teaspoon dried thyme
- 1 teaspoon dried oregano
- Salt and pepper to taste
- Fresh basil for garnish

INSTRUCTIONS

1. Preheat oven to 375°F (190°C). In the large, deep-bottom bowl, combine the eggplant, zucchini, yellow squash, bell peppers, onion, and garlic.
2. Add diced tomatoes, olive oil, thyme, oregano, salt, and crushed pepper. Toss to combine.
3. Transfer the mixture to the paper-arranged baking dish and spread evenly.
4. Bake for 27-30 minutes until the vegetables are tender. Garnish with fresh basil before serving.
5. Serve hot.

STUFFED ZUCCHINI BOATS

PREP TIME:
15 MINS

COOK TIME:
20 MINS

TOTAL TIME:
35 MINS

SERVING
4

Nutrition

Calories: 250, Protein: 18g,
Carbohydrate: 8g, Fat: 16g

INGREDIENTS

- 4 medium zucchinis, halved lengthwise
- 1/2 lb. ground turkey
- 1/2 cup diced tomatoes
- 1/4 cup diced onion
- 2 cloves garlic, minced
- 1/4 cup grated Parmesan cheese
- 1 tablespoon olive oil
- 1 teaspoon dried oregano
- Salt and pepper to taste
- Fresh parsley, chopped (for garnish)

INSTRUCTIONS

1. Preheat oven to 375°F (190°C). Scoop out the center of each zucchini half to create a boat shape. Set aside.
2. In a skillet, heat one tbsp oil over medium stove heat. Add chopped onion and mashed garlic and sauté until softened.
3. Add the ground turkey, diced tomatoes, oregano, salt, and crushed pepper. Cook until the turkey is done through.
4. Spoon the turkey mixture into the zucchini boats and place them on the paper-arranged baking sheet.
5. Sprinkle with grated Parmesan cheese. Bake for 15-20 minutes.
6. Garnish with fresh parsley before serving. Serve hot.

MEDITERRANEAN BEEF STEW

PREP TIME:
15 MINS

COOK TIME:
1.30 HOURS

TOTAL TIME:
1.45 HOURS

SERVING
4

Nutrition

Calories: 350, Protein: 25g,
Carbohydrate: 12g, Fat: 22g

INGREDIENTS

- 1 lb. beef stew meat, cubed
- 2 tablespoons olive oil
- 1 onion, diced
- 2 cloves garlic, minced
- 1 red bell pepper, diced
- 1 yellow bell pepper, diced
- 1 can (14 oz) diced tomatoes
- 1/2 cup beef broth
- 1 teaspoon dried oregano
- 1 teaspoon dried thyme
- Salt and pepper to taste
- Fresh parsley, chopped (for garnish)

INSTRUCTIONS

1. Heat two tbsp oil in a deep-bottom pot over medium stove heat. Add beef and brown on all sides. Remove and set aside.
2. Use the same pot and add chopped onion and mashed garlic. Sauté until softened. Add bell peppers and cook for another 3-4 minutes.
3. Return the beef to the pot. Add the diced tomatoes, beef broth, oregano, thyme, salt, and crushed pepper. Bring to a boil.
4. Decrease the stove heat, cover, and simmer for 1:30 hours until the beef is tender. Garnish with fresh parsley before serving. Serve hot.

BAKED COD WITH OLIVES AND TOMATOES

PREP TIME:
10 MINS

COOK TIME:
20 MINS

TOTAL TIME:
30 MINS

SERVING
2

Nutrition

Calories: 250, Protein: 24g,
Carbohydrate: 6g, Fat: 16g

INGREDIENTS

- 2 cod fillets
- 1 cup halved cherry tomatoes
- 1/2 cup pitted halved Kalamata olives
- 2 tablespoons olive oil
- 2 cloves garlic, minced
- 1 tablespoon lemon juice
- 1 teaspoon dried oregano
- Salt and pepper to taste
- Fresh parsley, chopped (for garnish)

INSTRUCTIONS

1. Preheat oven to 375°F (190°C). Place the cod fillets in the paper-arranged baking dish.
2. In a deep-bottom bowl, combine cherry tomatoes, olives, olive oil, garlic, lemon juice, oregano, salt, and crushed pepper. Mix well.
3. Spoon the tomato and oil-garlic mixture over the cod fillets. Bake for 20 minutes until the fish is done thoroughly and flakes easily.
4. Garnish with fresh parsley before serving. Serve hot.

STUFFED BELL PEPPERS WITH GROUND LAMB

PREP TIME:
15 MINS

COOK TIME:
30 MINS

TOTAL TIME:
45 MINS

SERVING
4

Nutrition

Calories: 300, Protein: 20g,
Carbohydrate: 10g, Fat: 20g

INGREDIENTS

- 4 bell peppers, halved and seeded
- 1 lb. ground lamb
- 1/2 cup diced tomatoes
- 1/4 cup diced onion
- 2 cloves garlic, minced
- 1/4 cup crumbled feta cheese
- 1 tablespoon olive oil
- 1 teaspoon dried oregano
- Salt and pepper to taste
- Fresh parsley, chopped (for garnish)

INSTRUCTIONS

1. Preheat oven to 375°F (190°C).
2. Heat one tbsp oil in a skillet over medium stove heat. Add chopped onion and mashed garlic and sauté until softened.
3. Add minced lamb, diced tomatoes, oregano, salt, and crushed pepper. Cook until the lamb is done thoroughly.
4. Spoon the lamb mixture into the halved bell peppers. Place the stuffed peppers in a paper-arranged baking dish and cover with foil.
5. Bake for 25 minutes. Remove the foil, sprinkle with feta cheese, and bake for more 5 minutes.
6. Spread parsley on top before serving. Serve hot.

KETO MEDITERRANEAN MEATLOAF

PREP TIME:
15 MINS

COOK TIME:
1 HOUR

TOTAL TIME:
1.15 HOURS

SERVING
4

Nutrition

Calories: 400, Protein: 28g,
Carbohydrate: 8g, Fat: 30g

INGREDIENTS

- 1 lb. ground beef
- 1/2 lb. ground lamb
- 1/2 cup almond flour
- 1/2 cup crumbled feta cheese
- 1/4 cup chopped fresh parsley
- 1/4 cup chopped red onion
- 2 cloves garlic, minced
- 2 large eggs
- 1 teaspoon dried oregano
- 1 teaspoon dried thyme
- Salt and pepper to taste

INSTRUCTIONS

1. Preheat oven to 375°F (190°C).
2. In the large, deep-bottom bowl, combine ground beef, ground lamb, almond flour, feta cheese, parsley, red onion, garlic, eggs, oregano, thyme, salt, and crushed pepper. Mix well.
3. Transfer the mixture to the paper-arranged loaf pan and shape it into a loaf.
4. Bake for one hour until the meatloaf is cooked through. Rest the meatloaf before slicing. Serve hot.

LEMON HERB ROASTED CHICKEN

PREP TIME:
15 MINS

COOK TIME:
1.15 HOURS

TOTAL TIME:
1.30 HOURS

SERVING
4

Nutrition

Calories: 450, Protein: 35g,
Carbohydrate: 2g, Fat: 32g

INGREDIENTS

- 1 whole chicken (about 4 lb.)
- 1/4 cup olive oil
- 2 tablespoons lemon juice
- 2 cloves garlic, minced
- 1 tablespoon dried oregano
- 1 tablespoon dried thyme
- Salt and pepper to taste
- 1 lemon, sliced
- Fresh rosemary and thyme sprigs (optional)

INSTRUCTIONS

1. Preheat oven to 375°F (190°C). In a small, deep-bottom bowl, mix olive oil, lemon juice, garlic, oregano, thyme, salt, and crushed pepper.
2. Rub the mixture all over the meat, including under the skin. If using, stuff the chicken cavity with lemon slices and fresh herb sprigs.
3. Place the chicken in a parchment paper-arranged roasting pan and roast for 1:15 hours. Rest the chicken for 10 minutes. Serve hot.

MEDITERRANEAN PORK TENDERLOIN

PREP TIME:
15 MINS

COOK TIME:
25 MINS

TOTAL TIME:
35 MINS

SERVING
4

Nutrition

Calories: 300, Protein: 25g,
Carbohydrate: 2g, Fat: 22g

INGREDIENTS

- 1 lb. pork tenderloin
- 1/4 cup olive oil
- 2 tablespoons lemon juice
- 2 cloves garlic, minced
- 1 tablespoon dried oregano
- 1 tablespoon dried rosemary
- Salt and pepper to taste

INSTRUCTIONS

1. Preheat oven to 400°F (200°C).
2. In a small, deep-bottom bowl, mix olive oil, lemon juice, garlic, oregano, rosemary, salt, and crushed pepper.
3. Rub the mixture all over the tenderloin meat. Put the skillet over medium stove heat and sear the tenderloin on all sides.
4. Transfer the pork to the paper-arranged baking dish and roast for 22-25 minutes. Rest the pork for 8-10 minutes before slicing. Serve hot.

GRILLED SARDINES WITH LEMON AND HERBS

PREP TIME:
10 MINS

COOK TIME:
10 MINS

TOTAL TIME:
20 MINS

SERVING
2

Nutrition

Calories: 250, Protein: 20g,
Carbohydrate: 1g, Fat: 18g

INGREDIENTS

- 8 fresh sardines, cleaned and gutted
- 1/4 cup olive oil
- 2 tablespoons lemon juice
- 2 cloves garlic, minced
- 1 tablespoon dried oregano
- Salt and pepper to taste
- Lemon wedges and fresh herbs for garnish

INSTRUCTIONS

1. Preheat the grill to medium-high heat.
2. In a small, deep-bottom bowl, mix olive oil, lemon juice, garlic, oregano, salt, and crushed pepper.
3. Brush the sardines with the olive oil mixture.
4. Grill the sardines for 3-4 minutes on one side until cooked thoroughly and charred. Serve with lemon wedges and fresh herbs. Serve immediately.

SNACK

ZUCCHINI FRITTERS WITH TZATZIKI SAUCE

 PREP TIME: 15 MINS

 COOK TIME: 15 MINS

 TOTAL TIME: 30 MINS

 SERVING 4

Nutrition

Calories: 250, Protein: 10g, Carbohydrate: 8g, Fat: 18g

INGREDIENTS

Zucchini Fritters:
- 2 medium zucchinis, grated
- 1/4 cup almond flour
- 1/4 cup crumbled feta cheese
- 2 large eggs
- 2 cloves garlic, minced
- 1 teaspoon dried oregano
- Salt and pepper to taste
- 2 tablespoons olive oil

Tzatziki Sauce:
- 1/2 cup Greek yogurt
- 1/2 cucumber, grated and drained
- 1 tablespoon lemon juice
- 1 clove garlic, minced
- 1 tablespoon fresh dill, chopped
- Salt and pepper to taste

INSTRUCTIONS

1. Place the grated zucchini in a towel (food grade or kitchen) and squeeze out as much moisture as possible.
2. In the large, deep-bottom bowl, combine the grated zucchini, almond flour, feta cheese, eggs, garlic, oregano, salt, and pepper. Mix well.
3. Heat two tbsp oil in a skillet over medium heat. Drop zucchini mixture (a spoonful) into the skillet and flatten slightly to form fritters.
4. Cook for 3-4 minutes for one side or until golden brown and cooked through. Remove and drain on the paper towels.
5. For the tzatziki sauce, combine Greek yogurt, grated cucumber, lemon juice, garlic, dill, salt, and pepper In a small deep-bottom bowl. Mix well.
6. Serve the zucchini fritters with tzatziki sauce on the side.

ALMOND AND OLIVE TAPENADE

PREP TIME:
10 MINS

COOK TIME:
00 MINS

TOTAL TIME:
10 MINS

SERVING
4

Nutrition

Calories: 180, Protein: 2g,
Carbohydrate: 4g, Fat: 18g

INGREDIENTS

- 1 cup mixed olives, pitted
- 1/4 cup almonds
- 2 cloves garlic
- 2 tablespoons olive oil
- 1 tablespoon lemon juice
- 1 tablespoon capers
- Salt and pepper to taste

INSTRUCTIONS

1. In a food blender, combine olives, almonds, mashed garlic, olive oil, lemon juice, and capers.
2. Pulse until the mixture is combined properly but still slightly chunky.
3. Powder it with salt and crushed pepper to taste. Serve immediately with veggie sticks or crackers.

SPICED NUTS AND SEEDS MIX

PREP TIME:
5 MINS

COOK TIME:
15 MINS

TOTAL TIME:
20 MINS

SERVING
4

Nutrition

Calories: 220, Protein: 6g,
Carbohydrate: 6g, Fat: 20g

INGREDIENTS

- 1/2 cup almonds
- 1/2 cup walnuts
- 1/4 cup pumpkin seeds
- 1/4 cup sunflower seeds
- 1 tablespoon olive oil
- 1 teaspoon smoked paprika
- 1/2 teaspoon ground cumin
- 1/2 teaspoon ground cinnamon
- 1/2 teaspoon salt
- 1/4 teaspoon cayenne pepper (optional)

INSTRUCTIONS

1. Preheat oven to 350°F (175°C).
2. In the large, deep-bottom bowl, combine the almonds, walnuts, pumpkin seeds, and sunflower seeds.
3. Drizzle one tbsp oil and sprinkle with smoked paprika, cumin, cinnamon, salt, and cayenne pepper if using. Toss to coat evenly.
4. Spread the mixture on the parchment paper-arranged baking sheet.
5. Bake for 12-15 minutes, stirring after the halftime has passed until the nuts and seeds are toasted and fragrant.
6. Let cool before serving.

CUCUMBER AND FETA BITES

PREP TIME:
10 MINS

COOK TIME:
00 MINS

TOTAL TIME:
10 MINS

SERVING
4

Nutrition

Calories: 100, Protein: 4g,
Carbohydrate: 4g, Fat: 8g

INGREDIENTS

- 1 large cucumber, sliced into rounds
- 1/4 cup crumbled feta cheese
- 1/4 cup Greek yogurt
- 1 clove garlic, minced
- 1 tablespoon fresh dill, chopped
- 1 tablespoon olive oil
- Salt and pepper to taste

INSTRUCTIONS

1. In a small, deep-bottom bowl, combine crumbled feta cheese, Greek yogurt, garlic, dill, olive oil, salt, and pepper. Mix well.
2. Place a small spoonful of the feta mixture onto each cucumber round. Arrange on the serving platter. Serve immediately.

SMOKED SALMON ROLL-UPS

PREP TIME:
10 MINS

COOK TIME:
00 MINS

TOTAL TIME:
10 MINS

SERVING
4

Nutrition

Calories: 120, Protein: 8g,
Carbohydrate: 2g, Fat: 9g

INGREDIENTS

- 4 ounces smoked salmon, sliced
- 1/4 cup cream cheese, softened
- 1 tablespoon fresh dill, chopped
- 1 tablespoon capers
- 1 tablespoon lemon juice
- 1/4 teaspoon black pepper

INSTRUCTIONS

1. In a small, deep-bottom bowl, combine cream cheese, fresh dill, capers, lemon juice, and black pepper. Mix well.
2. Spread cream cheese mixture (a thin layer) onto each slice of smoked salmon. Roll up the salmon slices and secure them with toothpicks if needed.
3. Arrange on the serving platter. Serve immediately.

MEDITERRANEAN DEVILED EGGS

PREP TIME:
15 MINS

COOK TIME:
10 MINS

TOTAL TIME:
25 MINS

SERVING
4

Nutrition

Calories: 120, Protein: 8g,
Carbohydrate: 2g, Fat: 9g

INGREDIENTS

- 6 large eggs
- 1/4 cup Greek yogurt
- 2 tablespoons crumbled feta cheese
- 1 tablespoon olive oil
- 1 tablespoon lemon juice
- 1 teaspoon Dijon mustard
- 1/2 teaspoon dried oregano
- Salt and pepper to taste
- 1 tablespoon chopped Kalamata olives (for garnish)
- Fresh parsley, chopped (for garnish)

INSTRUCTIONS

1. Place the eggs in a saucepan and cover with water. Bring to a boil, then decrease the stove heat and simmer for 10 minutes.
2. Drain and immediately throw into the cool water to stop the inside cooking. Peel the eggs and slice them in half lengthwise.
3. Remove the yolks and place them In a deep-bottom bowl.
4. Add Greek yogurt, feta cheese, one tbsp oil, lemon juice, Dijon mustard, oregano, salt, and pepper. Mash until smooth. Spoon the yolk mixture back into the empty egg white space.
5. Spread chopped Kalamata olives to garnish and fresh parsley.
6. Serve immediately.

AVOCADO HUMMUS

PREP TIME:
10 MINS

COOK TIME:
00 MINS

TOTAL TIME:
10 MINS

SERVING
4

Nutrition

Calories: 180, Protein: 4g,
Carbohydrate: 12g, Fat: 12g

INGREDIENTS

- 1 ripe avocado, peeled and pitted
- 1 can (15 oz weight) chickpeas, drained and rinsed
- 2 tablespoons tahini
- 2 tablespoons lemon juice
- 1 clove garlic
- 2 tablespoons olive oil
- Salt and pepper to taste
- 1/4 teaspoon ground cumin
- Fresh cilantro, chopped (for garnish)

INSTRUCTIONS

1. In a food blender, combine avocado, chickpeas, tahini, lemon juice, garlic, olive oil, salt, crushed pepper, and cumin. Blend until smooth.
2. Transfer to the serving bowl and spread fresh cilantro on top. Serve immediately with veggie sticks or pita chips.

PROSCIUTTO-WRAPPED ASPARAGUS

PREP TIME:
10 MINS

COOK TIME:
15 MINS

TOTAL TIME:
25 MINS

SERVING
4

Nutrition

Calories: 120, Protein: 6g,
Carbohydrate: 2g, Fat: 10g

INGREDIENTS

- 12 asparagus spears
- 6 slices prosciutto, halved lengthwise
- 1 tablespoon olive oil
- Salt and pepper to taste
- 1 tablespoon balsamic glaze (optional)

INSTRUCTIONS

1. Preheat oven to 400°F (200°C). Wrap asparagus spears (one by one) with a half slice of prosciutto.
2. Place the wrapped asparagus on the parchment-paper-arranged baking sheet, drizzle one tbsp oil, and sprinkle with salt and crushed pepper.
3. Bake for 12-15 minutes, until the prosciutto is crispy, and the asparagus is tender. Drizzle with balsamic glaze if desired. Serve immediately.

KETO ZUCCHINI CHIPS

PREP TIME:
10 MINS

COOK TIME:
2 HOURS

TOTAL TIME:
2.10 HOURS

SERVING
4

Nutrition

Calories: 80, Protein: 2g,
Carbohydrate: 4g, Fat: 7g

INGREDIENTS

- 2 medium zucchinis, thinly sliced
- 2 tablespoons olive oil
- 1/2 teaspoon salt
- 1/2 teaspoon paprika
- 1/4 teaspoon garlic powder

INSTRUCTIONS

1. Preheat oven to 225°F (110°C). Arrange the parchment paper-arranged baking sheet.
2. In a deep-bottom bowl, toss the zucchini slices with olive oil, salt, paprika, and garlic powder.
3. Arrange the zucchini slices in one layer on the paper-arranged baking sheet.
4. Bake for 2 hours, or until the zucchini slices are crispy, flipping halfway through.
5. Let cool before serving.

KETO GARLIC PARMESAN WINGS

PREP TIME:
10 MINS

COOK TIME:
40 MINS

TOTAL TIME:
50 MINS

SERVING
4

Nutrition

Calories: 350, Protein: 25g,
Carbohydrate: 2g, Fat: 26g

INGREDIENTS

- 2 pounds chicken wings
- 2 tablespoons olive oil
- 1/2 cup grated Parmesan cheese
- 4 cloves garlic, minced
- 1 teaspoon dried oregano
- 1 teaspoon dried basil
- Salt and pepper to taste
- 2 tablespoons chopped fresh parsley (for garnish)

INSTRUCTIONS

1. Preheat oven to 400°F (200°C). Arrange the parchment paper-arranged baking sheet.
2. In the large, deep-bottom bowl, toss the chicken wings with two tbsp oil, Parmesan cheese, garlic, oregano, basil, salt, and pepper until well coated.
3. Arrange the wings in one layer (don't overlap) on the prepared baking sheet. Bake for 35-40 minutes, turn the sides after halftime has passed until the wings are golden and crispy. Garnish with fresh parsley before serving.
4. Serve hot.

DESSERT

KETO BAKLAVA BITES

PREP TIME:
20 MINS

COOK TIME:
10 MINS

TOTAL TIME:
30 MINS

SERVING
8

Nutrition

Calories: 200, Protein: 4g,
Carbohydrate: 6g, Fat: 18g

INGREDIENTS

- 1 cup almond flour
- 1/4 cup melted butter
- 1/4 cup chopped walnuts
- 1/4 cup chopped almonds
- 1/4 cup chopped pistachios
- 2 tablespoons granulated erythritol
- 1 teaspoon cinnamon
- 1/4 cup melted coconut oil
- 1 teaspoon vanilla extract

INSTRUCTIONS

1. Preheat oven to 350°F (175°C). Arrange the muffin tin with paper liners.
2. In a deep-bottom bowl, mix almond flour, melted butter, erythritol, and cinnamon until well combined.
3. Press the mixture toward the bottom of each muffin liner to form a crust.
4. Use the other bowl to combine chopped walnuts, almonds, pistachios, melted coconut oil, and vanilla extract.
5. Spoon the nut mixture over the almond flour crust in each muffin liner. Bake for 10 minutes until golden and set. Allow to cool before serving.

DARK CHOCOLATE AND ALMOND BARK

PREP TIME:
10 MINS

COOK TIME:
10 MINS

TOTAL TIME:
20 MINS

SERVING
8

Nutrition

Calories: 150, Protein: 2g,
Carbohydrate: 5g, Fat: 12g

INGREDIENTS

- 1 cup dark chocolate chips (sugar-free)
- 1/2 cup chopped almonds
- 1 tablespoon coconut oil

INSTRUCTIONS

1. Melt the dark chocolate chips with one tbsp coconut oil in the heavy glass bowl using the double boiler or microwave, stirring until smooth.
2. Toss in the chopped almonds. Spread the mixture onto a parchment paper-arranged baking sheet. Chill for 1 hour (at least) until set. Break into pieces and serve.

GREEK YOGURT WITH HONEY AND WALNUTS

PREP TIME:
5 MINS

COOK TIME:
00 MINS

TOTAL TIME:
5 MINS

SERVING
2

Nutrition

Calories: 200, Protein: 10g,
Carbohydrate: 15g, Fat: 10g

INGREDIENTS

- 1 cup Greek yogurt
- 2 tablespoons chopped walnuts
- 1 tablespoon honey (or keto-friendly sweetener)

INSTRUCTIONS

1. Grab the two wide-mouth shallow bowls. Divide the Greek yogurt between the two bowls (use the wide mouth).
2. Drizzle each bowl with honey. Sprinkle with chopped walnuts. Serve immediately.

KETO LEMON BARS

PREP TIME:
15 MINS

COOK TIME:
30 MINS

TOTAL TIME:
45 MINS

SERVING
12

Nutrition

Calories: 200, Protein: 10g,
Carbohydrate: 15g, Fat: 10g

INGREDIENTS

Crust:
- 1½ cups almond flour
- 1/4 cup granulated erythritol
- 1/4 cup melted butter

Filling:
- 3 large eggs
- 1/2 cup granulated erythritol
- 1/2 cup fresh lemon juice
- 1 tablespoon lemon zest
- 2 tablespoons coconut flour

INSTRUCTIONS

1. Preheat oven to 350°F (175°C). Arrange the 8x8-inch baking pan with parchment paper.
2. In a deep-bottom bowl, mix almond flour, erythritol, and melted butter until well combined. Press the mixture softly toward the bottom of the prepared pan. Bake for 8-10 minutes, until the crust is lightly golden.
3. Use the other bowl and toss the eggs, erythritol, lemon juice, lemon zest, and coconut flour until smooth. Pour the filling over the pre-baked crust.
4. Bake for 20 minutes until the filling is set. Cool completely before cutting. Serve chilled.

ALMOND FLOUR BISCOTTI

PREP TIME:
15 MINS

COOK TIME:
30 MINS

TOTAL TIME:
45 MINS

SERVING
12

Nutrition

Calories: 110, Protein: 4g,
Carbohydrate: 3g, Fat: 9g

INGREDIENTS

- 2 cups almond flour
- 1/2 cup granulated erythritol
- 1 teaspoon baking powder
- 1/4 teaspoon salt
- 2 large eggs
- 1 teaspoon vanilla extract
- 1/2 teaspoon almond extract
- 1/2 cup chopped almonds

INSTRUCTIONS

1. Preheat oven to 350°F (175°C). Arrange the baking sheet with parchment paper.
2. In a deep-bottom bowl, combine almond flour, erythritol, baking powder, and salt.
3. Use the other shallow bowl, toss the eggs, vanilla extract, and almond extract. Add dry ingredients mixture and mix until the dough forms.
4. Fold in the chopped almonds.
5. Shape the dough into a log 12 inches long and 3 inches wide. Place on the paper-arranged baking sheet.
6. Bake for 25 minutes, until lightly golden. Remove and let cool for 10 minutes.
7. Decrease the oven heat to 300°F (150°C).
8. Slice the log into ½-inch thick slices. Arrange them on the paper-arranged baking sheet, cut side down. Bake for another 10-15 minutes until crisp. Let cool completely before serving.

CHOCOLATE AVOCADO MOUSSE

PREP TIME:
10 MINS

COOK TIME:
00 MINS

TOTAL TIME:
10 MINS

SERVING
4

Nutrition

Calories: 160, Protein: 2g,
Carbohydrate: 10g, Fat: 14g

INGREDIENTS

- 2 ripe avocados, peeled and pitted
- 1/4 cup unsweetened cocoa powder
- 1/4 cup granulated erythritol
- 1/4 cup almond milk
- 1 teaspoon vanilla extract
- Pinch of salt
- Fresh berries for garnish (optional)

INSTRUCTIONS

1. In a food blender, combine avocados, cocoa powder, erythritol, almond milk, vanilla extract, and salt. Blend on full power until smooth and creamy.
2. Divide the mousse between four serving dishes. Chill for 30 minutes (at least) before serving. If desired, garnish with fresh berries.

LEMON RICOTTA CAKE

PREP TIME:
15 MINS

COOK TIME:
40 MINS

TOTAL TIME:
55 MINS

SERVING
8

Nutrition

Calories: 220, Protein: 7g,
Carbohydrate: 5g, Fat: 18g

INGREDIENTS

- 1½ cups almond flour
- 1/2 cup granulated erythritol
- 1/2 cup ricotta cheese
- 1/4 cup melted butter
- 3 large eggs
- 1 tablespoon lemon zest
- 2 tablespoons lemon juice
- 1 teaspoon vanilla extract
- 1 teaspoon baking powder
- Pinch of salt

INSTRUCTIONS

1. Preheat oven to 350°F (175°C). Grease an 8-inch round cake pan.
2. In the large, deep-bottom bowl, combine almond flour, erythritol, baking powder, and salt.
3. In the other shallow bowl, toss ricotta cheese, melted butter, eggs, lemon zest, lemon juice, and vanilla extract.
4. Add the mixture of wet elements to the dry ingredients and mix until well combined. Drop batter into the prepared pan and smooth the top.
5. Bake for 35-40 minutes until is tooth-stick inserted and comes out clean. Let cool completely before serving.

KETO PUMPKIN PIE

PREP TIME:
15 MINS

COOK TIME:
45 MINS

TOTAL TIME:
60 MINS

SERVING
8

Nutrition

Calories: 200, Protein: 5g,
Carbohydrate: 8g, Fat: 18g

INGREDIENTS

Crust:
- 1½ cups almond flour
- 1/4 cup granulated erythritol
- 1/4 cup melted butter

Filling:
- 1 can (15 oz) pumpkin puree
- 3 large eggs
- 1/2 cup heavy cream
- 1/2 cup granulated erythritol
- 1 teaspoon vanilla extract
- 1 tablespoon pumpkin pie spice

INSTRUCTIONS

1. Preheat oven to 350°F (175°C). Grease a 9-inch pie dish. In a deep-bottom bowl, mix almond flour, erythritol, and melted butter until well combined.
2. Press the mixture softly toward the bottom of the prepared pie dish. Bake the crust for 10 minutes. Let cool.
3. In the other shallow bowl, toss pumpkin puree, eggs, heavy cream, erythritol, vanilla extract, and pumpkin pie spice until smooth.
4. Pour the filling into the pre-baked crust. Bake for 35-40 minutes or until the filling is set. Let cool completely before serving.

KETO CHOCOLATE FUDGE

PREP TIME:
10 MINS

COOK TIME:
5 MINS

TOTAL TIME:
15 MINS

SERVING
12

Nutrition

Calories: 150, Protein: 2g,
Carbohydrate: 5g, Fat: 14g

INGREDIENTS

- 1 cup unsweetened dark chocolate chips
- 1/2 cup coconut oil
- 1/4 cup almond butter
- 1/4 cup granulated erythritol
- 1 teaspoon vanilla extract
- Pinch of salt

INSTRUCTIONS

1. In a saucepan, melt the dark chocolate chips, coconut oil, and almond butter over low stove heat, stirring constantly until smooth.
2. Remove from heat and stir in erythritol, vanilla extract, and salt. Pour the mixture into a lined 8x8-inch baking dish and smooth the top.
3. Chill for 2 hours (at least) until set. Cut into squares before serving.

MEDITERRANEAN LEMON TART

PREP TIME:
20 MINS

COOK TIME:
30 MINS

TOTAL TIME:
50 MINS

SERVING
8

Nutrition

Calories: 180, Protein: 6g,
Carbohydrate: 6g, Fat: 16g

INGREDIENTS

Crust:
- 1½ cups almond flour
- ¼ cup granulated erythritol
- ¼ cup melted butter

Filling:
- 3 large eggs
- ½ cup granulated erythritol
- ½ cup fresh lemon juice
- 1 tablespoon lemon zest
- ¼ cup heavy cream

INSTRUCTIONS

1. Preheat oven to 350°F (175°C). Grease a 9-inch tart pan. In a deep-bottom bowl, mix almond flour, erythritol, and melted butter until well combined.
2. Press the mixture toward the bottom and up the sides of the prepared tart pan. Bake for 10 minutes, until lightly golden. Let cool.
3. Use the other shallow bowl, toss eggs, erythritol, lemon juice, lemon zest, and heavy cream. Pour the filling into the pre-baked crust.
4. Bake for 22-25 minutes until the filling is set. Let cool completely before serving.

One of the key aspects of successfully following the Keto-Mediterranean diet is having a well-structured meal plan. Planning your meals ahead of time helps you stay consistent, ensures you're getting the right balance of nutrients, and prevents the temptation to stray from your dietary goals. This section will guide you on creating a personalized meal plan, customizing it to fit your specific needs, and provide practical tips for staying on track.

Creating Your Meal Plan

Creating a meal plan for the Keto-Mediterranean diet involves choosing a variety of low-carb, nutrient-rich foods that align with the principles of both the ketogenic and Mediterranean diets. Here's how to create an effective meal plan:

Start with the Basics: Begin by planning your meals around core Keto-Mediterranean foods: lean proteins (like fish, poultry, and eggs), healthy fats (such as olive oil, avocados, and nuts), and low-carb vegetables (like spinach, zucchini, and bell peppers). Aim to include a balance of these components in each meal.

Plan for All Meals and Snacks: Outline what you'll eat for breakfast, lunch, dinner, and snacks. This comprehensive approach helps you avoid gaps in your nutrition and reduces the likelihood of making unhealthy choices out of convenience.

Incorporate Variety: To prevent boredom and ensure you get a range of nutrients, include different types of proteins, fats, and vegetables throughout the week. Try to rotate your meals and introduce new recipes regularly.

Consider Portion Sizes: Pay attention to portion sizes to manage your caloric intake and maintain ketosis. Use a kitchen scale or measuring cups to accurately measure your portions, especially when tracking macronutrients (fats, proteins, and carbs).

Use the 21-Day Meal Plan: If you're new to the diet, consider starting with the 21-day meal plan provided in this book. This structured plan will help you get accustomed to the diet, understand portion sizes, and discover which foods you enjoy the most.

Prep Ahead: Set aside time each week to prepare meals in advance. Cook large batches of proteins, chop vegetables, and make keto-friendly sauces or dressings. Store them in the fridge or freezer for quick and easy access throughout the week.

CUSTOMIZING MEAL PLANS TO YOUR NEEDS

Everyone's dietary needs and preferences are different, so it's important to customize your meal plan to suit your individual goals, lifestyle, and health conditions. Here's how you can personalize your Keto-Mediterranean meal plan:

Set Your Goals: Define what you want to achieve with the Keto-Mediterranean diet—whether it's weight loss, improved energy, better heart health, or managing a specific health condition. Your goals will guide the types of foods you include and the portion sizes you choose.

Adjust Macronutrient Ratios: Depending on your activity level and personal needs, you may need to adjust the ratio of fats, proteins, and carbohydrates. For example, athletes might require more protein, while those focused on deep ketosis might reduce carbs even further.

Accommodate Dietary Restrictions: If you have allergies or intolerances (e.g., lactose intolerance, gluten sensitivity), make sure to replace those ingredients with suitable alternatives. For example, use almond milk instead of cow's milk, or coconut flour instead of wheat flour.

Fit Your Lifestyle: If you have a busy schedule, prioritize quick and easy recipes that don't require extensive preparation. Look for meals that can be made in one pot or batch-cooked and stored for later use.

Monitor and Adjust: Pay attention to how your body responds to the diet. If you feel sluggish or notice you're not losing weight, consider adjusting your portion sizes or the types of foods you're consuming. Everyone's metabolism is different, so it may take some time to find what works best for you.

Include Favorite Foods: Incorporate your favorite Keto-Mediterranean foods into your meal plan. Enjoying the foods you love will help you stay committed to the diet and avoid feelings of deprivation.

21-DAY MEAL PLAN

This 21-day meal plan is designed to help you seamlessly integrate the Keto-Mediterranean diet into your daily life. The meal plan includes a variety of delicious and nutrient-dense recipes that align with the principles of both ketogenic and Mediterranean diets. The plan is structured to provide balanced meals that promote healthy weight loss, improved energy levels, and overall well-being.

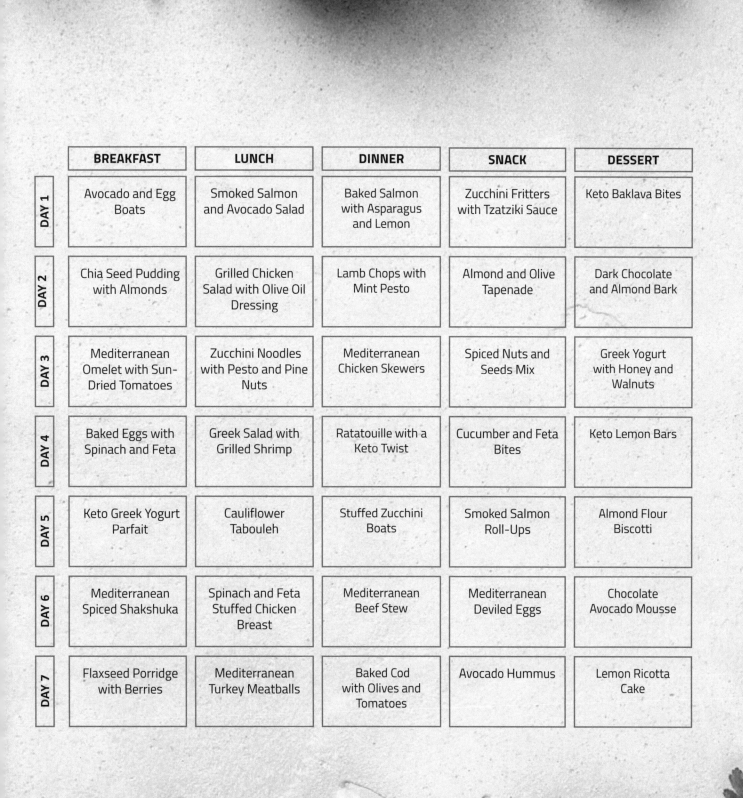

	BREAKFAST	LUNCH	DINNER	SNACK	DESSERT
DAY 1	Avocado and Egg Boats	Smoked Salmon and Avocado Salad	Baked Salmon with Asparagus and Lemon	Zucchini Fritters with Tzatziki Sauce	Keto Baklava Bites
DAY 2	Chia Seed Pudding with Almonds	Grilled Chicken Salad with Olive Oil Dressing	Lamb Chops with Mint Pesto	Almond and Olive Tapenade	Dark Chocolate and Almond Bark
DAY 3	Mediterranean Omelet with Sun-Dried Tomatoes	Zucchini Noodles with Pesto and Pine Nuts	Mediterranean Chicken Skewers	Spiced Nuts and Seeds Mix	Greek Yogurt with Honey and Walnuts
DAY 4	Baked Eggs with Spinach and Feta	Greek Salad with Grilled Shrimp	Ratatouille with a Keto Twist	Cucumber and Feta Bites	Keto Lemon Bars
DAY 5	Keto Greek Yogurt Parfait	Cauliflower Tabouleh	Stuffed Zucchini Boats	Smoked Salmon Roll-Ups	Almond Flour Biscotti
DAY 6	Mediterranean Spiced Shakshuka	Spinach and Feta Stuffed Chicken Breast	Mediterranean Beef Stew	Mediterranean Deviled Eggs	Chocolate Avocado Mousse
DAY 7	Flaxseed Porridge with Berries	Mediterranean Turkey Meatballs	Baked Cod with Olives and Tomatoes	Avocado Hummus	Lemon Ricotta Cake

	BREAKFAST	LUNCH	DINNER	SNACK	DESSERT
DAY 1	Greek-Inspired Scrambled Eggs	Tuna and Olive Salad	Stuffed Bell Peppers with Ground Lamb	Prosciutto-Wrapped Asparagus	Keto Pumpkin Pie
DAY 2	Lemon Ricotta Pancakes	Lemon Herb Chicken Salad	Keto Mediterranean Meatloaf	Keto Zucchini Chips	Keto Chocolate Fudge
DAY 3	Prosciutto-Wrapped Asparagus with Eggs	Shrimp and Avocado Salad	Lemon Herb Roasted Chicken	Keto Garlic Parmesan Wings	Mediterranean Lemon Tart
DAY 4	Keto Cauliflower Breakfast Hash	Mediterranean Cauliflower Couscous	Mediterranean Pork Tenderloin	Zucchini Fritters with Tzatziki Sauce	Keto Baklava Bites
DAY 5	Avocado and Egg Boats	Smoked Salmon and Avocado Salad	Grilled Sardines with Lemon and Herbs	Almond and Olive Tapenade	Dark Chocolate and Almond Bark
DAY 6	Chia Seed Pudding with Almonds	Grilled Chicken Salad with Olive Oil Dressing	Ratatouille with a Keto Twist	Spiced Nuts and Seeds Mix	Greek Yogurt with Honey and Walnuts
DAY 7	Mediterranean Omelet with Sun-Dried Tomatoes	Zucchini Noodles with Pesto and Pine Nuts	Stuffed Zucchini Boats	Cucumber and Feta Bites	Keto Lemon Bars

	BREAKFAST	LUNCH	DINNER	SNACK	DESSERT
DAY 1	Baked Eggs with Spinach and Feta	Greek Salad with Grilled Shrimp	Lamb Chops with Mint Pesto	Smoked Salmon Roll-Ups	Almond Flour Biscotti
DAY 2	Keto Greek Yogurt Parfait	Spinach and Feta Stuffed Chicken Breast	Baked Cod with Olives and Tomatoes	Mediterranean Deviled Eggs	Chocolate Avocado Mousse
DAY 3	Mediterranean Spiced Shakshuka	Mediterranean Turkey Meatballs	Keto Mediterranean Meatloaf	Avocado Hummus	Lemon Ricotta Cake
DAY 4	Flaxseed Porridge with Berries	Tuna and Olive Salad	Stuffed Bell Peppers with Ground Lamb	Prosciutto-Wrapped Asparagus	Keto Pumpkin Pie
DAY 5	Greek-Inspired Scrambled Eggs	Lemon Herb Chicken Salad	Lemon Herb Roasted Chicken	Keto Zucchini Chips	Keto Chocolate Fudge
DAY 6	Lemon Ricotta Pancakes	Shrimp and Avocado Salad	Mediterranean Pork Tenderloin	Keto Garlic Parmesan Wings	Mediterranean Lemon Tart
DAY 7	Prosciutto-Wrapped Asparagus with Eggs	Mediterranean Cauliflower Couscous	Grilled Sardines with Lemon and Herbs	Zucchini Fritters with Tzatziki Sauce	Keto Baklava Bites

TIPS FOR STAYING ON TRACK

Staying on track with the Keto-Mediterranean diet requires dedication and mindful habits. Here are some practical tips to help you remain consistent and committed to your health goals:

Keep a Food Journal: Write down everything you eat and drink each day. Tracking your meals can help you stay accountable, identify patterns or triggers that lead to unhealthy eating, and monitor your progress.

Plan Ahead for Challenges: Anticipate situations where you might be tempted to stray from your diet, such as social events, holidays, or dining out. Plan ahead by eating a Keto-Mediterranean meal before you go, bringing a keto-friendly dish to share, or researching menu options beforehand.

Stay Hydrated: Drink plenty of water throughout the day to stay hydrated and support your body's metabolic processes. Proper hydration also helps control hunger and cravings.

Listen to Your Body: Pay attention to your hunger and fullness cues. Eat when you're hungry and stop when you're satisfied, not overly full. This mindful eating approach helps prevent overeating and promotes a healthy relationship with food.

Find Support: Connect with others who are following the Keto-Mediterranean diet. Join online communities, support groups, or find a buddy who shares your goals. Having support can keep you motivated and provide encouragement during challenging times.

Celebrate Small Wins: Recognize and celebrate your progress, no matter how small. Whether it's losing a few pounds, feeling more energetic, or making it through a challenging week without straying from your plan, acknowledge your achievements and use them as motivation to keep going.

Be Patient and Persistent: Remember that lasting results take time. Be patient with yourself and understand that there may be setbacks along the way. Stay persistent, learn from any mistakes, and keep moving forward.

Stay Educated: Continue learning about the Keto-Mediterranean diet, nutrition, and healthy living. Staying informed will empower you to make better food choices and maintain your commitment to the diet.

By creating a personalized meal plan, customizing it to fit your needs, and following these tips, you can successfully adopt the Keto-Mediterranean diet and enjoy its many health benefits. Whether you're looking to lose weight, boost your energy, or improve your overall well-being, these strategies will help you stay on track and achieve your goals.

DINING OUT AND SOCIAL EVENTS

Following the Keto-Mediterranean diet doesn't mean you have to avoid dining out or miss out on social events. With a little planning and knowledge, you can enjoy restaurant meals and gatherings while staying true to your dietary goals. This section provides practical tips for navigating restaurant menus, identifying Keto-Mediterranean-friendly dishes, and handling social gatherings and holidays without feeling deprived.

Navigating Restaurant Menus

When dining out, the variety of choices can be overwhelming, but knowing what to look for can make the experience enjoyable and diet-friendly. Here are some tips for navigating restaurant menus while following the Keto-Mediterranean diet:

Start with the Protein: Look for dishes that feature lean proteins such as grilled chicken, fish, shrimp, or steak. These are often the main components of Keto-Mediterranean meals. Request these proteins grilled, baked, or sautéed, and avoid options that are breaded, fried, or served with heavy sauces that may contain hidden carbs.

Request Substitutions: Don't hesitate to ask for substitutions to make your meal more Keto-Mediterranean-friendly. For example, replace high-carb sides like pasta, potatoes, or bread with steamed vegetables, a side salad, or extra avocado. Most restaurants are happy to accommodate dietary requests.

Choose Healthy Fats: Ensure your meal includes healthy fats, such as olive oil, avocado, or nuts. Ask for olive oil and vinegar for your salad dressing instead of creamy, high-sugar dressings. You can also request a slice of avocado or a handful of nuts as an additional side.

Focus on Low-Carb Vegetables: Select dishes that include or allow you to add a variety of low-carb vegetables like spinach, broccoli, zucchini, or bell peppers. These vegetables align with the Mediterranean focus on fresh, nutrient-dense ingredients.

Avoid Hidden Sugars and Carbs: Be cautious of sauces, marinades, and dressings, which may contain added sugars or hidden carbohydrates. Ask for these on the side so you can control the amount you use. Stick to simple seasoning with herbs, spices, and lemon juice.

Skip the Bread Basket: Politely decline the bread basket or chips when dining out. If others at your table are enjoying these items, focus on your water or ask for a small starter, such as a side of olives or a small green salad.

Check the Appetizer Section: Appetizers often include smaller portions and can be excellent Keto-Mediterranean options. Look for items like grilled octopus, shrimp cocktail, smoked salmon, or a cheese plate with nuts.

Keto-Mediterranean Friendly Dishes to Look For

While navigating the menu, keep an eye out for dishes that naturally fit the Keto-Mediterranean diet. Here are some examples of what to look for:

- **Grilled Fish or Seafood:** Dishes like grilled salmon, shrimp skewers, or seafood salads are typically prepared with olive oil and served with vegetables, making them excellent choices.
- **Salads with Protein:** Opt for a hearty salad topped with grilled chicken, salmon, shrimp, or steak. Include plenty of low-carb vegetables, olives, feta cheese, and avocado. Ask for dressing on the side and choose olive oil and vinegar.
- **Greek or Mediterranean Platters:** These often feature a combination of meats, cheeses, olives, and vegetables. Look for platters that include grilled meats, tzatziki, hummus (in moderation), and fresh vegetables.
- **Steak or Chicken with Vegetables:** A classic option that fits well within the diet. Make sure the dish is served with steamed or grilled vegetables instead of starchy sides.
- **Egg-Based Dishes:** Omelets, frittatas, and eggs Benedict (without the muffin) can be good choices, especially for breakfast or brunch. Add vegetables, cheese, and avocado to make the dish more satisfying.
- **Kebabs and Skewers:** Look for grilled meat or vegetable skewers served with a side of salad. These are often seasoned with herbs and spices rather than sugary sauces.

Tips for Social Gatherings and Holidays

Social events and holidays can be challenging when you're trying to stick to a Keto-Mediterranean diet. However, with some preparation and strategic choices, you can enjoy these occasions without compromising your goals: Bring a Keto-Mediterranean Dish: If you're attending a potluck or gathering, offer to bring a dish that aligns with your diet. This ensures you have at least one option that fits your dietary needs. Consider bringing a fresh salad with olive oil dressing, a platter of grilled vegetables, or a cheese and nut tray.

- **Eat Before You Go:** If you're unsure about the food that will be served, have a small Keto-Mediterranean meal or snack before leaving. This will help curb your hunger and make it easier to avoid high-carb temptations.
- **Focus on Protein and Vegetables:** When at a buffet or party, fill your plate with protein options like grilled chicken, seafood, or meat. Add low-carb vegetables or a salad, and skip the bread, pasta, and desserts.
- **Stay Hydrated:** Drinking water can help control hunger and prevent overeating. Opt for water or sparkling water with lemon instead of sugary drinks or alcohol. If you choose to drink alcohol, select a dry wine or a spirit mixed with soda water.
- **Be Mindful of Portions:** It's easy to overeat when surrounded by an abundance of food. Use a smaller plate, take smaller portions, and eat slowly to savor each bite. This helps you stay aware of your intake and prevents overindulgence.
- **Politely Decline:** It's okay to say no to foods that don't fit your diet. Be polite but firm, and explain that you're following a specific eating plan. Most people will respect your decision.
- **Enjoy the Company:** Remember that social gatherings are about more than just food. Focus on enjoying the company of friends and family, engaging in conversations, and participating in activities. Shifting your focus away from food can make it easier to stick to your diet.

Dining out and attending social events can be enjoyable and diet-friendly with the right strategies. By learning to navigate restaurant menus, choosing Keto-Mediterranean-friendly dishes, and following tips for social gatherings and holidays, you can stay committed to your health goals while still enjoying the social aspects of eating. With preparation and mindfulness, you can make choices that align with your Keto-Mediterranean lifestyle, no matter where you are.

MAINTAINING A BALANCED LIFESTYLE

Following the Keto-Mediterranean diet is a crucial step toward improving your health and well-being, but achieving optimal health requires more than just focusing on what you eat. A balanced lifestyle that includes regular exercise, effective stress management, adequate sleep, and proper hydration is essential for maximizing the benefits of the Keto-Mediterranean diet. This section provides practical advice on integrating these key components into your daily routine.

Exercise Recommendations

Regular physical activity is a vital part of a balanced lifestyle and works synergistically with the Keto-Mediterranean diet to enhance overall health. Exercise not only supports weight loss but also improves cardiovascular health, boosts energy levels, enhances mental clarity, and promotes a positive mood. Here are some exercise recommendations to complement your Keto-Mediterranean diet:

- **Aerobic Exercise (Cardio):** Incorporating moderate-intensity aerobic exercise into your routine can help improve heart health, increase stamina, and burn fat. Activities like brisk walking, cycling, swimming, and jogging are excellent options. Aim for at least 150 minutes of moderate-intensity aerobic activity per week, which can be broken down into 30-minute sessions, five days a week.

- **Strength Training:** Building and maintaining muscle mass is important for metabolic health and can help increase fat burning. Strength training exercises like weight lifting, resistance band workouts, bodyweight exercises (such as push-ups, squats, and lunges), and Pilates should be included at least two to three times a week. Focus on working all major muscle groups for a balanced approach.

- **Flexibility and Balance Exercises:** Activities that enhance flexibility and balance, such as yoga and tai chi, are beneficial for reducing the risk of injury, improving posture, and promoting relaxation. Incorporate these activities into your routine a few times a week to complement your cardio and strength training efforts.

- **High-Intensity Interval Training (HIIT):** HIIT involves short bursts of intense activity followed by periods of rest or low-intensity exercise. This type of workout is effective for burning fat and improving cardiovascular fitness. Incorporate HIIT sessions once or twice a week to boost your workout routine.

- **Active Lifestyle:** In addition to structured exercise, aim to stay active throughout the day. Simple activities like taking the stairs, going for a walk during lunch breaks, gardening, or playing with your kids can increase your overall activity level and contribute to better health.

Managing Stress

Chronic stress can negatively impact your health and undermine the benefits of the Keto-Mediterranean diet. High stress levels can lead to hormonal imbalances, increased inflammation, poor sleep, and unhealthy eating habits. Managing stress is essential for maintaining a balanced lifestyle and supporting overall well-being. Here are some effective stress management techniques:

Mindfulness and Meditation: Practicing mindfulness or meditation can help calm the mind, reduce anxiety, and improve emotional resilience. Spend a few minutes each day focusing on your breath, meditating, or practicing mindfulness exercises. Apps and guided meditation sessions can be helpful for beginners.

Physical Activity: Exercise is a natural stress reliever that releases endorphins, the body's feel-good hormones. Regular physical activity can help reduce stress, improve mood, and boost energy levels. Choose activities you enjoy, whether it's dancing, hiking, or yoga, to make exercise a fun and effective way to manage stress.

Deep Breathing Exercises: Deep breathing techniques can help activate the body's relaxation response. Practice deep, slow breathing by inhaling through your nose for a count of four, holding your breath for four counts, and exhaling through your mouth for a count of four. Repeat this cycle several times to reduce tension and promote relaxation.

Time Management: Organizing your day and setting realistic goals can reduce stress and prevent feelings of overwhelm. Prioritize tasks, set boundaries, and learn to say no when necessary. Taking control of your schedule can help you manage stress more effectively.

Social Support: Connecting with friends, family, or support groups can provide emotional support and reduce stress. Sharing your thoughts and feelings with someone you trust can be comforting and help you feel understood and supported.

Hobbies and Relaxation: Engage in activities that bring you joy and relaxation, whether it's reading, painting, gardening, or listening to music. Taking time for yourself to unwind and do something you love can significantly reduce stress levels.

The Importance of Sleep and Hydration

Adequate sleep and proper hydration are fundamental to maintaining a balanced lifestyle and supporting the benefits of the Keto-Mediterranean diet. Both sleep and hydration play crucial roles in overall health, affecting everything from metabolism and energy levels to cognitive function and mood.

Sleep

Why Sleep Matters: Quality sleep is essential for the body's repair and recovery processes. It helps regulate hormones, supports immune function, and improves cognitive performance. Lack of sleep can lead to increased stress, poor decision-making, and a higher risk of chronic health conditions such as obesity, diabetes, and heart disease.

Sleep Recommendations: Aim for 7-9 hours of quality sleep per night. Establish a consistent sleep schedule by going to bed and waking up at the same time every day, even on weekends. A regular sleep routine helps regulate your body's internal clock.

Creating a Sleep-Friendly Environment: Make your bedroom a relaxing, sleep-friendly space. Keep it cool, dark, and quiet. Use comfortable bedding and invest in a good mattress and pillows. Consider using blackout curtains and white noise machines if necessary.

Sleep Hygiene Tips: Avoid caffeine and heavy meals before bedtime. Reduce screen time and exposure to blue light from phones, computers, and TVs at least an hour before bed. Engage in calming activities like reading, taking a warm bath, or practicing relaxation techniques before sleep.

Hydration

Importance of Hydration: Proper hydration is vital for maintaining energy levels, supporting metabolism, regulating body temperature, and promoting healthy digestion. It also aids in nutrient absorption and helps flush out toxins from the body.

Daily Water Intake: Aim to drink at least 8-10 cups (64-80 ounces) of water per day, more if you are physically active or in a hot climate. Carry a water bottle with you throughout the day to encourage regular drinking.

Signs of Dehydration: Be aware of signs of dehydration, such as dry mouth, fatigue, headaches, dizziness, and dark-colored urine. If you notice these symptoms, increase your water intake immediately.

Hydrating with Electrolytes: On the Keto-Mediterranean diet, your body may lose more electrolytes due to the diuretic effect of ketosis. Consider incorporating electrolyte-rich drinks, such as water with a pinch of salt and lemon or commercially available electrolyte tablets, to maintain proper balance.

Hydration Tips: Flavor your water with slices of citrus fruits, cucumber, or mint to make it more enjoyable. Drink a glass of water before each meal to aid digestion and help control hunger.

Maintaining a balanced lifestyle through regular exercise, effective stress management, adequate sleep, and proper hydration is crucial for maximizing the benefits of the Keto-Mediterranean diet. By incorporating these elements into your daily routine, you can enhance your overall health, support weight management, and improve your quality of life. Remember, a healthy lifestyle is about balance and making choices that support your well-being, both physically and mentally.

Thank you so much for purchasing this book and embarking on your journey with the Keto-Mediterranean diet. I truly appreciate your support and hope that the recipes, tips, and meal plans provided will help you achieve your health and wellness goals. Your feedback is invaluable, and I would be incredibly grateful if you could take a moment to leave a review on Amazon. Your review not only helps me improve but also assists other readers in discovering the benefits of this lifestyle.

Thank you again for your trust, and happy cooking!

CONCLUSION

As you reach the end of this journey into the Keto-Mediterranean diet, take a moment to reflect on the wealth of information, recipes, and lifestyle tips that you have explored. By choosing to adopt this powerful combination of ketogenic and Mediterranean eating principles, you are embracing a healthier, more balanced way of life that supports not only weight loss but also long-term wellness and vitality.

The Keto-Mediterranean diet offers a sustainable, enjoyable approach to eating that is rich in healthy fats, lean proteins, and nutrient-dense vegetables. By following the meal plans, customizing them to your personal needs, and staying active and hydrated, you are setting yourself up for success. This diet isn't just a temporary change—it's a lifestyle that fosters heart health, mental clarity, energy, and longevity.

Remember, the key to thriving on this diet lies in consistency, adaptability, and mindful choices. Be patient with yourself, celebrate your progress, and continue to explore new foods and recipes that excite you. Use the tools and knowledge you've gained from this book to make informed decisions that support your health goals. Whether you're cooking at home, dining out, or enjoying a social gathering, you now have the confidence to make choices that align with your Keto-Mediterranean lifestyle.

Here's to delicious meals, improved health, and a lifetime of well-being. You've made an incredible commitment to your health—now enjoy the journey!

Made in United States
Troutdale, OR
12/28/2024

27384001R00049